# Dialectic, Rhetoric and Contrast

The Infinite Middle of Meaning

**Richard Boulton**

St George's, University of London;
Kingston University

**Series in Philosophy**

VERNON PRESS

www.vernonpress.com

*In the Americas:*
Vernon Press
1000 N West Street, Suite 1200
Wilmington, Delaware, 19801
United States

*In the rest of the world:*
Vernon Press
C/Sancti Espiritu 17,
Malaga, 29006
Spain

Series in Philosophy

Library of Congress Control Number: 2021931318

ISBN: 978-1-64889-375-9

Also available: 978-1-64889-149-6 [Hardback]; 978-1-64889-265-3 [PDF, E-Book]

Cover designed by Aurelien Thomas.

# Table of contents

Introduction     v

Chapter I     **Method**     1

Dialectic and Rhetoric     1

Validating a Concept Spectrum     12

Chapter II     **Sense**     17

Emotion     17

Rationality     23

The Absolute     29

Truth     34

Value     39

Chapter III     **Essence**     47

Meaning     47

Narrative     51

Patterns and Problems     57

Existence     61

Contrast     66

Chapter IV     **Consequence**     73

Life     73

Mind and Body     77

Human     84

The Individual     91

Rules and Exceptions     97

Conclusion                                   107

References                                   117

Index                                        129

# Introduction

This book is the result of a thought experiment inspired by the methods of dialectic and rhetoric. The experiment takes the meaning of singular words through a repeating pattern, firstly a word is opposed (through antonym), and then the two words are synthesised together into a middle word between the two, then the synthesised concept is opposed, and the pattern repeats. Rather than continuing endlessly, or becoming exhausted, I argue that the meanings of the words uncovered become recursive. The words that I have experimented with can be traced through up to 12 iterations before returning to their original meaning. This is not to suggest some sort of constant or absolute principle, but rather as a means to demonstrate how meaning can be understood as recursive by using dialectic on a manageable number of concepts up to 12. The book speculates on the consequences that this conjecture may have for metaphysics and current theories of meaning.

***

The discord between dialectic and rhetoric has perpetuated throughout the ages from classical philosophy into our current epoch. Plato's (2004) adoption of dialectic pits Socrates as heroically countering the evils of sophism, relativism and self-interest, by adopting dialectic; a form of reasoning based upon a dialogue of arguments and counter-arguments to bring about a reasoned resolution of the argument or improvement of the dialogue. At first, it would seem as if the benefits of dialectic were obvious, that dialectics offers a way to assert 'reason' as superior.

In such a process, however, with the hindsight of a history of problematic idealistic examples, and the albescence of a fully accepted complete and coherent encyclopaedia of categories (such as the one attempted in outline only by Hegel, 2015), no one end point can ever be asserted with confidence. For as soon as one dialogue has concluded there is nothing inherent to the process to stop another opposing dialectic becoming ready to take its place. Consequently, as dialectical debate unfolds it unavoidably employs rhetoric as its medium to reason a debate into more or less persuasive arguments. This means that dialectic can never fully forefront rhetoric, as at its most rudimentary rhetoric demonstrates that any one reason must always have an alternative or exception.

This implies that the conclusions reached by either dialectic or rhetoric are just as relevant yet unresolvable today as they have always been. Neither one is closer to being superseded when Aristotle first asserted that 'rhetoric is the counterpoint to dialectic' in the opening to his treatise on rhetoric (Aristotle, 2012). However, if both methods are coherent as well as contradictory they each pose a problem to the result of the other. Either rhetoric/dialectic are part of a bigger set of guiding principles we do not yet know, or dialectic and rhetoric are both in some way inaccurate and do not point to any one consistent 'reason' at all. In some ways, the problem between the two reflects the problems of the assertion of all knowledge.

The history of philosophy is littered with such arguments that, when aggregated, resort to such simple dualisms (e.g. rhetoric v dialectic, or mind v body; subject v object; man v nature). When discussions become polarised, they demand the same conclusion as that above; either to find an alternate solution or to abandon the initial argument altogether. The act of refuting or affirming dualisms cannot avoid forming another a dualism even when aware of the process and expressly trying not to do so. For example, if one side argues against the simplification of dialogue into dualisms, it enables an opposing position eager to discover exactly how much can be represented dualistically through binary. With the advent of the digital revolution contemporary thought has little choice but come to terms with the ability of binary algebra to represent all information in simple Boolean, binary mathematics (for examples see Gunkel, 2007; Hui, 2016; Burckhardt and Höfer, 2017). Attempts to counter the effects of binary fit into a longer lineage of traditions in cultural theory that seek to counter the reduction of knowledge to hierarchical dualisms. Eminent examples such as Baudrillard's (1994) Simulacra; or Derrida's Deconstruction; or Deleuze's (1983) Rhizome present concepts exemplifying the dangers of dualisms in the study of culture. Post-structuralism more generally can be typified as the attempt to allay the binary reductions caused by scientific cultures (and an explicit denial of dialectic). In their antagonism however, interpretations following in the footsteps of these theories have been helpless to perpetuate the same dualistic and reductive approach against the natural sciences that these theories have sought to counter.

Running counter to these movements, McLuhan's (2001) famous euphemism that 'the medium is the message' has demonstrated and expertly developed sophisticated understandings of rhetoric, but full employment of rhetoric as a rigorous and scholarly method has always been subject to some caution. This is because at its most extreme, rhetoric represents purposeful manipulation. The task of contending the effects of rhetoric has been indispensable to resisting religious dogma since the renaissance (as can be seen in the accounts of Valla and Agricola discussed in Mack, 1993). Nevertheless, the formal study of rhetoric still continues to evolve and recent developments like the philosophy of communication serve to demonstrate its relevance (see Mangion, 2011; or Chang and Butchart, 2012). In some shape or form, the existence of rhetoric in any discourse is unavoidable. The persistence of rhetoric has resulted in a variety of disparate attitudes towards truth across the entire human sciences, and the inability to resolve such controversies has been used to corroborate claims affirming the superiority of the natural sciences as beyond such questions of rhetoric (see Pickering and Guzik, 2009). In response contemporary movements in contemporary human sciences have little choice but to defend some sort of partial position towards the natural sciences, initiating questions as to whether they cumulatively build towards a distinct disciplinary logic or are simply reactionary to other more dominant forms of knowledge production (Mannheim, 2015; Scheler, 2013). This has produced a number of well-versed dialogues in contemporary theory between endorsements or denouncements of modern science and culture or some position between the two thereby re-initiating dualism on top of dualism in a back and forth fashion (the "science wars" is a good example of this, see Labinger and Collins, 2001). In all these disciplinary dynamics, all sides employ dialectic and rhetoric, but the exact line between where each one would fall is highly contested.[1]

Of great requisite therefore would be a method that could consolidate dialectic and rhetoric equally without resorting to one side of a dualism or disavowing oppositions and distinctions between categories altogether (i.e. a commonality that doesn't invite any further schism between dominating disciplines). The reason why these discussions are so insurmountable is because their controversies reflect the root of logic itself. It would seem that on some scale, all creation can be represented to be within a binary of 0 (nothing) and 1 (everything). This presents a (negative existential) problem because when presented in extreme terms they are in opposition, yet how can nothingness and everything really be opposed without each cancelling out the meaning of the other? If either everything or nothing were on their own true, either concept would obscure the other and all other meanings. Put another way, if everything can be represented by a 0 or a 1, then nothing else apart from 0 or 1 would really mean anything. This means that considering either nothing or everything as inherently true is problematic. Inherited from classical logic (via Aristotle) are the three Laws of Thought; two of which are important here: the law of non-contradiction and the law of the excluded middle (Hamilton et al., 1860). They state that contradictory propositions cannot both be true in the same sense at the same time. There are a number of possible options for resolving the negative existential proposed above (for example antimony, unity of opposites, perspectivism or dialetheism). However, as any refutations still lead back to contradiction at some point, the interpretation of these principles still preoccupy contemporary thought as a result. Classical examples such as the Liar's Paradox or Epicurus's trilemma pose as much fascination today as they always have done.

In contrast, as physics proposes ever more advanced theories of relativity, uncertainty, chaos; or as Gödel's (1931) Incompleteness theorem, or modal logic demonstrate their importance in mathematics and computing, none of these theories has proven to be strictly bound to classical logic as they demonstrate logical contradictions and inconsistencies. Consequently, contemporary thought wishing to stay abreast of such innovations have found it difficult to find a position between classical logic and scientific advancement. For any philosophical perspective to overcome this would require a way to access the meaning of a contradiction beyond the contradiction it poses to itself, or put another way meaning beyond logic, or a meaning beyond its own meaning (see "meaning" as presented by Arnett and Holba, 2012). Both rhetoric and dialectic engage with contradiction by presenting a way to conceive of something outside of the opposition contradiction poses to itself. This means that opposition is key to both methods but is used to different ends; if dialectic uses opposition to prove the point, rhetoric uses opposition to prove the exception (a point raised in both Jeffries, 2011; and Davies, 2014). The development of this line of enquiry requires a more thorough investigation of the meaning of opposition. Consequently, the account here seeks to explore oppositions meaning at its most direct and elemental. In language, the formal expression of opposition is in the form of antonym and many lexical categorisations exist around the specific features and uses of antonym (see Cruse, 2001 for a good overview). What is harder to demonstrate however, is how the opposition in antonym is sensed, experienced and constituted. For instance, from what sense does the appreciation of opposition derive, is opposition located independently to individual experience, or is it dependent upon it?

This feeds into a familiar theme in philosophy attributed to Kant's (2001) demonstration of the impossibility of detaching appearance from 'things-in-themselves'. Since publication (almost 250 years ago) this theme has been central to the development of philosophy. Rather than tread this very well-worn philosophy towards idealism, however, I wish to divert it to argue that antonym represents something extra-ordinary to any interpretation, logic, reason or sense. For example, antonym can be considered as both a reference to something else whilst at the same time always its own unique kind of thing. In other words, each antonym is specific to the concepts it represents whilst being identical in some sense to all other antonyms. As a result, an antonym is both doing the job of referencing whilst also constituting the object that is being referenced. This means that antonym is directly related to the experience of relationality itself (which is significant because relationality is the conduit of meaning, thought and experience). This points to some kind of apeiron behind antonym we could call opposition. However, the concept of opposition applied to antonym is only one expression of a much more meaningful experience. To conceptualise such an apeiron requires an acknowledgement of opposition that spans many distinctions and meanings, not only directly as in contradiction but the condition with which all things perceivable contrast in general, so cannot be represented accurately so narrowly defined. This means that the method can be used to develop meaning that is extra-linguistic.

This point can be further demonstrated by considering contrast; i.e. the state by which one thing stands out from another. Without contrast, the awareness of any object, thought, feeling or state would be indistinct and non-experienceable, and so knowledge of all things relies upon contrast in some way. All things measured must refer to contrast as their medium. However, when considering the location of contrast, an infinite scale is evoked as contrast shifts dependent upon the scale used to measure the contrast. The exact point where two objects meet is impossible to define exactly. As a result, contrast does not get entangled in the same difficulties of defining 'things-in-themselves' as it is at the cusp of perception, neither fully part of the perceiver nor fully external (or independent), rather it is in an infinite abstraction between the two, and across all the senses (contrast demonstrates an intimate infinity we can access but never entirely possess). When considering the relationship between things as relative, the contrast is absolute and vice versa. Contrast has no lack of coverage, for example, it was the basis of Locke's (1998) Essay Concerning Human Understanding (most specifically in reference to 'the paradox of the basins'), published in 1689 and vital to the development of philosophy and empiricism in all sciences. However, most (Locke included) would consider contrast as a point of passage – in Locke's case to argue the emptiness of mind without experience – and not a destination. In reference to Locke, once contrast is considered as both innate to mind whilst also external it denies a full gone conclusion on the origin of perception, and so here I propose to shift focus to investigate the contrast itself. The sticking point therefore, is that once identified, how can contrast be distinguished to account for all of its many manifestations? Contrast can be compared to the concept of the infinite which is contradictory from a finite perspective. Even though the distinction between things can be labelled as contrast, it would be reductive to reduce it just to that alone, as from contrast all known differences emanate. For the sake of argument here I will describe this apeiron[2] as contrast, but it can also be closely related to antonym and contradiction (as more symmetrised), or opposition more generally (but should represent just about anything that can be made distinct even categories that are complementary to each other). The challenge therefore, is to devise a method to explore this notion of contrast without forcing contrast to take on any one concept in particular.

As dialectic and rhetoric represent two attitudes towards looking at the opposition, I propose that combining the two will serve to provide a more ingrained meaning of contrast. I will refer to this combination as simply the method of rhetoric dialectic. Such a name is constituted because the method I will propose resembles dialectic, but wishes to exemplify the aspects of rhetoric most often obscured by strict adherence to dialectic. Specifically, this will mean averting the assertion that dialectic has an end state, pointing instead to an adoption of dialectic in continuum. Such an understanding of dialectic must concede that any conclusions (or synthesis) reached has an exception and within that exception lies rhetoric (my account also doesn't consider dialectic as being driven by any absolute concept such as reason, contradiction, nothingness or negation which are integral to interpretations of idealism and Hegel, instead the concept of contrast is used as a means to avoid posing a force at the centre of dialectic). For this reason, if the style of method employed has to have a specific referent it should avoid being categorical. In keeping with long-established traditions, the method could be named the rhetoric dialectic method or even rhetorical dialecticism. However, it is imperative to emphasise here that neither one should hold rank over the other. Rhetoric dialectic, dialectic rhetoric in effect it matters not which way around they are as (will be argued) they are an opposite direction towards the same solutions (Eemeren, 2002). Therefore, the title of 'rhetoric dialectic' should offer reference to both traditions whilst not overemphasising its position or originality. The name serves to both place the method proposed in a tradition whilst conceding that its definition and meaning should remain in contention and open to challenges.

This is not to suggest, however, that the method proposed does not have some specificities and differences concerning both rhetoric and dialectic. Most specifically, its focus is on the concepts behind individual words as the smallest unit of meaning and the building blocks of argument rather than on the resolution of whole arguments (or histories as in Hegel). Defining what constitutes a concept is as contested as the study of the mind itself, as concepts are an integral component to the study of mind (see Margolis and Laurence, 2015). Rather than affirm any one specific definition I wish to maintain a degree of scepticism towards the way that the word 'concept' is evoked to fulfil empirical or rationalist agendas. From an empirical standpoint, the general thrust of these debates argue that the mind is a blank slate, conversely, debates from a rationalistic standpoint argue that there is some internal force or impulse guiding sense. There is no end of mediated approaches to language acquisition which could also be cited here.[3] But any attempting to fix a firm position, necessarily forms an opposing standpoint towards alternate positions. Therefore, in wishing to see beyond dualisms, I wish to strip the connotations gathered by these debates over the centuries from the word 'concept' to approach it as free from any one singular research tradition as possible. Here 'concept' has a very specific usage (which is not meant to be exhaustive) to denote a meaning that has a direct and clear antonym. A certain amount of ambiguity will always accompany antonym as it ironically represents both a relation and an opposition. The aim here is to isolate antonyms to concepts with opposing meanings that are as symmetrical as possible. Rather than suggest that concepts are merely smaller versions of arguments, I will demonstrate the extent to which concepts can be considered as distinct and free from the inference they gain when adopted into an argument.

The method is explored using themes developed in relation to western metaphysics, but should be of relevance to disciplines across the social sciences and humanities, as well as impossible to untangle from epistemology, semantics or hermeneutics. This is to open the method out to the broadest interpretation, whilst also recognising the imprudence of asserting a new method into controversial disciplinary politics prematurely, before investigating its meaning.

This task however, is made more difficult by the status of metaphysics being somewhat obscured in contemporary philosophy. Following the concerns of scientific methodologies and early 20th century figures such as Carnap (1932) or Heidegger (1997), individual thoughts and feelings are understood to be able to only ever reflect upon their own experience, and so no words can originate from which to begin to founder metaphysical principles (in contrast to physical ones). The effect of which has been a general falling out of favour with the concept of metaphysics in the major trends of continental philosophy. Whilst similar concerns have also been shared by analytic philosophy committed to discussing anti-realism in lieu of metaphysics (Braver, 2007). Harman (2018) highlights that attitudes to metaphysics have (unjustly) developed pejorative naïve or mystical associations, and goes on to argue that the term ontology is regarded as more rigorous and respectable so proposes using the two terms as synonyms. I do not wish to dismiss these cautions entirely, but highlight the direction they are committed to. In such a schema 'being' (consigned to individual things) and 'existence' (encompassing all things) also become interchangeable, which results in a denigration of the scope of metaphysics by implying a limited access to existence only through being and not vice versa. Such a distinction has been divisive in philosophy with the continued rise of modern science, as science (and empiricism) puts in conflict the essence and authenticity of individual thought against external truths. The idea of knowledge as independent to the individual that has accompanied the development of modern science makes implicit the ways that individual thoughts and actions are the subject to inherent biases and limitations (Kahn, 1982).

Therefore, I do not wish to dispute that thought is reliant upon being for reflection of existence, I wish to take a different tact to question the evidence that thought is anything more or less than that which it observes. Rather than looking for existence in actual things or words, I will look for it by speculating on what lies between all things allowing them to contrast each other. As argued, contrast cannot be said to belong to either the individual or externally to them, and so, such a view of contrast could be said to be a direct (and indirect) experience of existence (rather than merely 'being' alone). This makes necessary an understanding of meaning and sense as not exclusive to logic, but to be found in all sensations, emotions and feelings capable of appreciating contrast. The result will be to posit a new perspective 'in-between' that sees contrast as both related to what is observed (i.e. physical) but always aside from it at the same time.[4] Such a position is in excess of, or extra to observable physical objects, and so the only way to describe such a contradictory perspective is with metaphysics. It is acknowledged that such an enquiry into meaningfulness cannot banish the mystical any more than it can fideism (Sartwell, 1992). My understanding of metaphysics implies that there is always something alternative (or an exception to any rule) to any interpretation (unlike ontology which is only concerned with a being as a certainty of factuality). Being and existence are not opposed, rather they are two ways of looking at the same thing, being as inward and sensual/emotional and existence as outwards and logical (evidence for this will be discussed throughout this account). To draw on metaphysics is therefore inherently useful to give an insight into contrast.

***

The interpretation of the method poses a number of challenges to existing fields of expertise and disciplinary divisions. However, any challenges made are not for their own sake, each observation disseminated in the book is centred upon the method, and the structure never strays far from this method. The discussion here develops a notion of contrast as a means to distinguish connotation from broader meaning, or in other words to initiate a way of thinking with as little outside influence as possible. Ironically, contrast, opposition and antonym, the quintessence of duality are employed here as a way to avoid binary thinking, and so in this sense contrast becomes like Plato's (2005) pharmakon; both poison and remedy. This is reminiscent of Derrida (2017), for whom all writing is a form of pharmakon. For Derrida, any description of a duality is logocentric and can never refer to anything but language itself. Derrida's position is more extreme than my own, I acknowledge the self-referent character of antonym but use it rather differently to loop back on and self-affirm the original meaning. Such an affirmation points to more than the meaning behind the words and can be used as a basis to speculate on similarities in the sensation of contrast across all senses and cognitions. This highlights an important distinction in my approach, the issues raised in this account are not with the concept of binary per se (or any other concept), but with the assertion that any one concept or logic alone is ever able to demonstrate the entirety of that which it represents (this is the premise of the semantics initiated by Korzybski, 1933).[5] When any concept is represented it creates its own contrast which opens up new possibilities for interpretations always one step ahead of itself. Consequently, as logic is only able to access one concept at any one time any logical inference will always have an exception. I argue that to describe something as the result of one logic or perspective alone is a form of idealism as such an explanation necessarily excludes other explanations that contradict it.

Idealism presents philosophy with thrill and despair in equal measure. The extent to which mind and matter interrelate has always been a major lure of philosophical interest, and contemporary philosophy has proven no exception. According to Meillassoux (2009) all philosophies working under the influence of Kant inadvertently work towards (what he calls) a correlation between interpretation and our access to the world as existent independent to the individual. The main impetus of this distinction is to escape from trends of philosophy since the mid-20th century that have prohibited truths aside from the subject. The difficulty of maintaining such a position is to demonstrate meaning outside of language whilst avoiding absolute idealism, i.e. to avoid the view of seeing ideals as the origin and pre-requisite of material phenomena. Such endeavours are important as no such universally accepted position has ever been posited with which to founder any one point of view as being anything other than one particular, individual perspective. To maintain that any one perspective is the one and only true perspective is to place it over and above that which it is describing (and such a process is idealistic). In response to this, I argue that all that can ever be sensed is contrast.[6] Contrast is both intimate and external, it sets aside where both the subject and object begin and end and outlines the separation between all things. Therefore, contrast is not fully personal (or ideal), and it is also not fully material, so it is irrelevant whichever way such a distinction is argued as both distinctions are necessary and evidence that neither one is the truth and the whole truth alone.

My definition of idealism therefore is extremely loose, no interpretation can be seen to be free of idealism entirely any more than something idealistic can be viewed as free of reality (and of special interest are the concept of nothing, everything and infinity that imply absolute ideals). Rather than isolated to specialist philosophical discussion, to believe in such a definition also implies that the most ardent of realists are also idealistic. This is precisely the point, concepts are inherently ideals, and therefore idealism is totally intractable from meaning. To fully eliminate such a view therefore would require a perspective that is completely counter-intuitive, to believe in ideas whilst not believing in them. Or to believe in what is meant without believing meaning. This is not to imply absolute idealism however, as the ability to use meaning to imply non-meaning is precisely that which makes it possible to pose the question in the first place. Ideals must rely on whatever is not idealistic for definition, which in this case must be realism. For example, all that is not idealism must be that which reacts against our interpretation of it. In the words of Philip K Dick: 'reality is that which, when you stop believing in it, doesn't go away' (Dick, 1988). Therefore, the only recourse to see beyond idealism is from that which contrasts it, such contrast comprises not ideals but the sense of contrast itself. My perspective therefore, attempts to avoid seeing the traditional lines between idealism v realism, or empiricism v rationalism as exclusive and instead attempt to access their full inter-relationality.

As a result, my account attempts to avoid resorting to singular explanations by analysing from the point of view of contrast. This task is extremely paradoxical however, for no sooner has an explanation been rendered in contrast than it becomes a new contrast which must be opposed. So, to attempt this is to attempt a seemingly impossible position (a position always just out of reach); to think a thought that accommodates all its negations, whilst also being able to navigate and distinguish between these diverse ranges of thought without descent into meaninglessness. In this way, those who equate philosophy with consistency may be frustrated with this account. I would rather the achievements of my account be measured in the level of coherence brought to the subject incoherence. The account is attempting to tread the same contradictory path that forges meaning against meaninglessness (Priest, 2006a).

To this end, I attempt to assess the method free of one particular school or tradition (other than more generally reflecting the concerns of continental thought). This is perhaps in contrast to trends in contemporary scholarship that have professionalised to become more and more specific on their respective subject matters. When breaking with tradition the difficulty lies in seeing all of the implications immediately, and any explanations can branch into several established traditions that threaten to quickly extinguish the impetus of possible new directions. Rather than pit my account against a list of heroes and villains I have sought to uncover the meaningfulness of the resources used even if in opposition to each other. Many of the ideas exemplified by the method I propose here are very old and established and have no exhaustion of long and extensive tomes that tease out the nuance and detail of their respective subject matter. As a result, my account covers a lot of heavily populated ground very quickly. The justification for which is that much of the structure and order is led by the method in dialogue with traditional rhetorical/dialectical concerns, i.e. each section is based around one use of the method, and a consequent table, subsequent questions raised by these tables then form the basis for the next table. No section strays far from an explanatory table. The tables supporting my account are approximations, and some people may contend with my compilation or interpretation, or cultural perspective. My aim is not to create a series of static tables charting a series of absolute relations between concepts, rather I am seeking to question the intuition which allows me to find the opposites to concepts in the first place and why concepts are recursive. Therefore, it is with humility and caution that I present this method as a means to postulate new lines of philosophical enquiry rather than a site of 'once and for all' definitions of concepts. What is presented here therefore should be seen as something that is iterative and ongoing rather than static.

Both rhetoric and dialectic are formalised terms to describe tools freely used and employed by all (whether intentionally or not). Their strength lies in their ability to allow an exception. Perhaps this gives my account an ambiguous perspective on its own argument (arguing whilst attempting to not take a position). Given the dynamics of how the method proceeds and the aims and objectives of compiling such a method encompassing both dialectic and rhetoric, this is perhaps inevitable. The method purposively abstains from being used as a way to prove things as indisputably true or false, and works towards a metaphysics able to encompass all meanings including all truth and fallacy in the same universe whilst not flattening meaning out into a monism where meaning becomes meaningless or where one meaning alone comes to mean everything. As a result, I have gone to painstaking lengths to not denounce entirely anything that can be meaningfully posed, just as my approach is to avoid fully endorsing one truth alone. To most scholarly practice focused on discourse this may seem to banish argument entirely and so be completely illogical and meaningless. But it is precisely this that sustains the argument. Rather exasperatingly, not arguing constitutes an argument, as an argument must always contrast something, once posed one must always have a position towards an argument. This is the bemusement with which I am hoping the reader will tolerate when beginning to read the book, suspending judgment until fair assessment can be given.

The book has been split into four sections which explore the method from the specific to the broad, the first defines the method, the second demonstrates the connection between thought, feeling, sense and contrast, the third meanings ambiguous relationship to matter, and the forth on the contrasting position of the individual as distinct from its surroundings. Together they form a metaphysical exploration that relates sense, meaning, thought and its physical opposition together.

## Endnotes

[1] For similar reasons Schrag (2003) argues that rhetoric is the means by which philosophy and social practices and communications in their widest sense are intertwined and implicate each other.

[2] Calling this an apeiron gets right to the crux of the matter as it is not to assume that I am trying to describe contrast as preeminent and a monism like in Anaximander. Or assume that contrast is the same as Heraclitus' or Hegel's unity of opposites, i.e. that two opposites are co-instantiated in at least one object and vice versa. Contrast cannot exist without two objects of which it is opposed to, and so it is both preeminent to objects and creating an effect like a force whilst wholly isolated to and dependent on individual objects at the same time. No object can substantiate contrast, yet none can escape it either.

[3] In particular the interactionist theory initiated by Vygotsky which adds no end of nuance between the two see edited volume of Pablé (2017).

[4] The foundations of such a viewpoint can be explored in de Man (2013) and Shklar (2004) in reference to the hermeneutic loop. They argue that to understand interpretation as circular places perspective in a position that is only ever illusively between two other things.

[5] Korzybski devised a model of semantics that demonstrated that the process of making sense of an environment is one of abstraction, and that any abstractions made leave out many characteristics of the original stimuli. This implies that language can never exhaust (or categorise) all of the properties of its environment.

[6] Debates about what constitutes 'sense' spans the entirety of philosophy, as do considerations of where each sense begins and ends. Here I do not wish to limit these debates as Heller-Roazen (2007) demonstrates even knowing or unknowing could be considered as a sense.

Chapter I

# Method

## Dialectic and Rhetoric

This book seeks to develop a method that reveals the contrast between the meaning of concepts. This contrast is impossible to situate definitively as its existence and significance can only be demonstrated in relation to something else. As a result, research methods will not be presented in the style of an external lens drafted in to answer a fixed research question, as is so often portrayed. This is because an exterior analytical perspective obscures a view of the contrast generated from its own application. Rather, of utmost importance is that the method proposed, and the findings implied preserve the contrast from which they derive meaning. Therefore, what is emphasised is how the method, research question and findings are inter-related and imply each other. I.e., the method will be used to generate findings on subjects that help to explore the workings of the method itself. The concession for employing this approach is that a succinct, neatly bound or exhaustive answer to my research question (on contrast) via methods is not possible. On the contrary, the methods employed will be used generatively to point to further meanings and problems.[1]

To explore contrast, I will employ the concept of a spectrum, for which I will put forward a precise definition. Principally, a spectrum cannot be conceived as a simple range or scale, it should imply a continuum. Thus concepts that can be said to form a spectrum should be arranged so that their meanings are in a loop that is accurately gradated through a symmetrical range of values. Such a spectrum should offer a range of interconnected values that share an exact and relationship that compliment as much as confound each other.

The closest existing endeavours to render concepts to a spectrum can be traced to the methods pioneered by Euler, Venn or logical graph theory (Venn, 2014; Peirce, 1976). Graphs such as the Venn and Euler diagrams (closely related to set theory) are diagrammatic means of representing sets (which can be related to concepts) and their logical relationships. Such endeavours differ from a spectrum, however, as their results demonstrate several poles with a central position in the centre. A spectrum on the other hand would demonstrate a gradation of concepts in a continuum implying no centre (as first demonstrated by Isaac Newton 1671). The difference can be demonstrated with practical examples such as the political spectrum, notable versions would be

Eysenck's political chart or the Nolan chart (Eysenck, 2000; Nolan, 1971). Such charts have at their base a matrix, and so are compiled around two axes. This differs from a spectrum however, as a spectrum would imply a gradation around a circle in continuum with no distinct pole and where all concepts are equal. Attempts to make a gradation with a formal logic struggle to justify authoritatively the positioning of categories. It could be argued therefore, that concepts are dissimilar to the spectrums seen in the effects of energy like the electromagnetic spectrum, and that the concepts of physics are the wrong lens with which to view meaning.

When observed during the various trials of neuroscience, the brain can be seen to engage large networks of neurons with electromagnetic activity. In the patterns produced thought and concepts can be correlated to the matter and energy that is observed when individuals are thinking. However, when it comes to providing a deeper explanation of how what is observed is related to the experience of the thoughts themselves, these observations are inconclusive. The formal name for this problem is called 'the hard problem of consciousness' (Chalmers, 1995) (discussed further in section 3). It refers to a paradox in thought that questions the ability of mechanistic description to explain consciousness as experienced. Such investigations are forced to concede therefore, that although consciousness may be associated to physics in some way, there is some uncertainty as to whether the link between matter and consciousness could ever be fully explained by neuroscience. To avoid this dilemma, rather than go from the outside in therefore, i.e. trying to equate observable matter to consciousness, it makes more sense to start from the inside, i.e. to determine what makes meanings distinguishable from one another.

At its most broad this search is as old as philosophy itself (known as the problem of universals Plato, 1987a). For example, if we take an object (the classic example being that of two cups), how can the similarity of them be traced over two iterations, what exactly constitutes their similarity? Does the similarity only exist in interpretation or do similar objects have some actual shared property? An easy retort would be to argue that there are no such shared properties and that physical objects are merely collectives of more elementary particles or part of something more immense. However, the same question could be applied to the similarities between elementary particles or the similarities of immense things to their constituent parts. Any meaning must assume some similarities; otherwise, no distinction could be asserted. Over the centuries many propositions have attempted to engage this problem (for example, in the last 100 years we could consider the universals posed by set theory in mathematics; the structuralism of Levi-Strauss; or the archetypes of the collective unconscious as posed by Jung; the theory of universal grammar by Chomsky), but none have succeeded without evoking counter claims for being regressive, leaving something aside, or exterminating all meaningful distinction completely. Any postulation of a universal similarity cannot escape being self-fulfilling. For example, to assert a similarity must also imply a difference and vice versa or else such a similarity/difference would be indistinguishable from its surroundings. The process of distinction therefore merely produces more and more objects (which can be analogised to the problem of induction or Gödel's incompleteness theorems). As a result, I will take a different tact on the problem. Rather than look at objects for a universal I will assert that that which is common to both is at the exact point where things become what they are and are not i.e. through contrast.[2] I will use this to evoke a dialectics not perpetuated by negation but by contrast. Rather than root dialectic in the mysterious concept of nothingness, I will attempt to evoke no root at all other than the contrast posed between different concepts. Therefore, rather than assume contradiction as inherent and pre-emptive of meaning, I employ contrast as a means to define opposites or antonyms between concepts as that which eclipses their meaning. The goal of this method will be to create a spectrum of dialectic where each concept symmetrically contrasts the other until they form a closed loop.

***

Asserting that it is possible to plot concepts as a spectrum implies that meaning is in some way infinite. However, the number of words that exist in any language is not infinite (as readily affirmed in morphology). Therefore, words, concepts and the meanings behind them must be divergent; for example, words can be broken down into smaller units such as morphemes, or can have several forms under one lexeme, and as such, words carry connotations that change meanings and concepts over time.[3] A spectrum of words alone has the potential to be misleading as the concepts behind them change.[4] Any resulting spectrum will, to a certain extent be an approximation as it must use words whilst acknowledging their temporal access to express meaning. Just as any dictionary or thesaurus can only define words prescriptively or descriptively against the actual usage of any language. To reiterate, my aim is not to create a series of tables that chart a series of absolute relations between concepts, rather I am seeking to question the intuition which allows me to find the opposites to concepts in the first place and why concepts become recursive. The starting point for defining concepts will be with the contrast between opposing words, rather than rely on the words themselves (which have many connotations that can alter their meaning Chase, 1966). This follows the semiotics first introduced by Saussure (1964) that understands meaning to derive from the relationship between the contrasts in language.[5] I wish to use this point to imply that the contrast between words are the origin and regulator of their meanings and should therefore be considered as preceding the words used to represent them.[6] In the same way, a prism separates light, the method here seeks to function as a prism to separate specific meanings from contrast.

**Figure I-1**

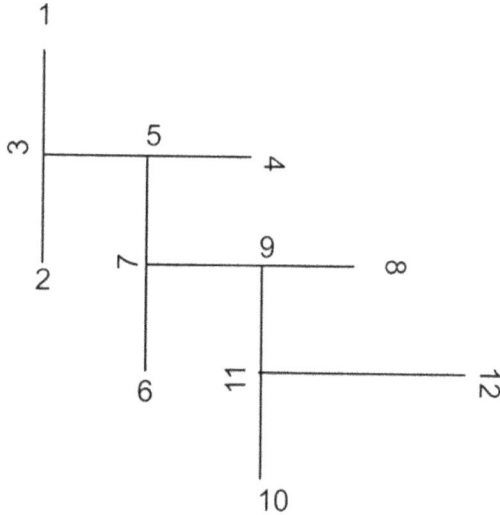

For most words, a direct opposite can be very readily found using a dictionary to form a dualism. Once a dualism is formed between two concepts, it becomes possible to relate them to a third position placed at the exact middle point between the first two opposing positions. The middle position should both affirm as well as negate the first two positions (like the way that red and blue mixed result in purple and not red + blue).[7] This can be compared to the dialectical method, where two oppositions are combined into a synthesised third, but here the concept produced implies no superiority as dialectic traditionally does when synthesising argument. The meaning of this middle position should imply both polar oppositions as well as have its own distinction. Once the third position in the middle of the first two concepts has been established a position for a fourth concept then becomes possible opposite to the third, middle position. The fourth position should be the opposite of the third position. Which then creates the space for a fifth position between the third and fourth positions following the same rule used to create the third. The method can then continue to uncover concepts as oppositional or between two oppositions indefinitely. Through following this method however, and employing an experimental process of trial and error, I argue (and will demonstrate below) that the meaning for many words can be considered to be recursive after 12 iterations (to reiterate, this is not to suggest some sort of constant or absolute principle, but rather as means to demonstrate how meaning can be understood as recursive by using dialectic on a manageable number of concepts up to 12). Above is a diagram which demonstrates the order in which the method proceeds to create positions for concepts (for the sake of clarity I will refer to this a fractal diagram as it is meant to represent the division of meanings into fractures).

Whilst clearly reminiscent of dialectic there are also some important distinctions, the emphasis here is not to produce an end-point but a continuum of related concepts.[8] Therefore, the method detailed here seeks to instil rhetoric to divert the process away from a critical end-point or all-encompassing reason to search instead for the exception in a concept through its opposite to produce a continuum. Rather than producing an argument where each preceding thesis trumps the thesis which has come before the emphasis here has shifted here to produce a set of concepts where each concept becomes roughly equal to one another in the same continuum. Compared to a binary 0 and 1 (or Boolean's operators of AND, OR, NOT), the oppositions in meaning uncovered using this method must always be considered to contain a qualitative difference distinct from any other definition. The potential of this method is that from any meaning with a direct opposition is possible to make a whole spectrum of concepts.

To test the method, the first concept attempted should be the main contention of both rhetoric and dialectic; i.e. logic (the definitions given are my own but using the Oxford English Dictionary for support).

## Emotion (2)

If logic is the first concept on the diagram, the first task becomes to find its opposite, which in this case is emotion. Emotion is opposed to logic as emotion is the sensation of experiencing something independently of logical understanding.

## Intuition (3)

Between logic and emotion must come a concept that combines both their meanings whilst also having its own distinct and separate meaning. The concept of intuition fulfils this criterion as intuition is the unique sensation of experiencing something beyond both emotion and logic.

## Instinct (4)

The opposite of intuition is instinct, which is the ability to act innately without reflexive thought or feeling.[9] Instinct could be depicted as unthinking, but here instinct could also be understood as a sensation which occurs independent of emotion, logic and intuition, and so sensing something whilst not being aware of experiencing it. The existence of an instinct therefore is only comprehendible in retrospect.

### Inference (5)

Intuition and instinct bridge the gap between sensual experiences which are and are not conscious. The method of reaching a conclusion on something for which the individual has a limited sense of is a process of inference.[10] The process of inference detaches intuitive from instinctual understandings until what results is something which becomes comprehensive.

### Imagination (6)

Imagination is in opposition to inference as rather than being a process of excluding intuitive or instinctual understandings, imagination is the process of drawing on them to form new sensations or experiences.

### Delusion (7)

Between inference and imagination is delusion, which could include dreams and hallucinations. Delusion constitutes an awareness of something that is incoherent with an individual's other senses.

### Awareness (8)

The opposite of delusion is awareness, which is the sensation of having a coherent sense of awareness, or a capacity for accurate cognition.

### Interpretation (9)

The middle between delusion and awareness is the process by which one can be worked out from the other, and that process is one of interpretation. Interpretation is the sense of putting together things already known, with the proviso that there may be more than one way to put the information together.

### Calculation (10)

The opposite to interpretation is calculation, which is also the process of putting information together, however, unlike interpretation calculation holds in it that there is only one coherent way in which to put the information together.

## Literal Thinking/Denotation (11)

In between interpretation and calculation is the sensation that something is literal, i.e. that it is an authentic singular thing. This is when interpretation and calculation of something result in the same conclusion. This could also be understood in terms of analogy.

## Abstract Thinking/Connotation (12)

The opposite to literal thinking is abstract thinking, which can also be understood as connotation or metaphor, which is contrasted against literal thinking as abstract thinking seeks to find similarities in thinking rather than authenticity or singularity. As Aristotle (1996) confers, 'metaphor implies an intuitive perception of the similarity in the dissimilar'.[11]

## Logic (1)

Of significance at this stage is that the diagram becomes a loop as the meaning in the middle between a literalism and a connotation is logic. Logic is the process of working out the literal from the connotative and reflects the process by which the mind processes sensations. Consequently, the diagram now makes a continuous spectrum, and the 12 concepts taken together form a set of relations (note: a single concept may inform more than one word or vice versa, and so meanings should be cross-referenced as much as possible throughout the whole process).[12]

When put into the diagram, the set looks like this:

**Figure I-2**

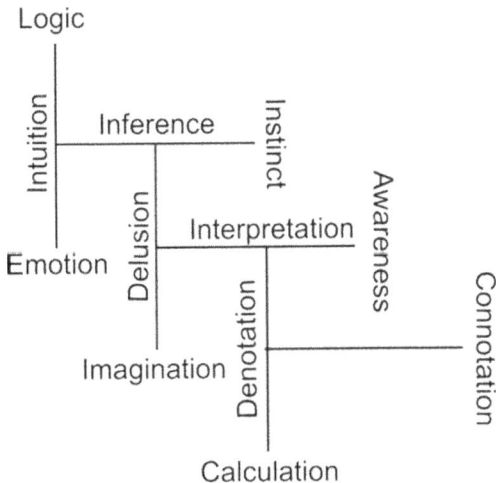

The model that has been created can be compared to the methods of persuasion, ethos, pathos and logos in Aristotle's (2012) 'Rhetoric'. For example, pathos could be compared to emotion, logos to logic and ethos to intuition. Although the sequence now goes further, and 11 other concepts (12 in total) can now be related to logic. All of these concepts could also be understood as modes of persuasion similar to Aristotle's, however, they also detail something broader around how thought is processed. It could be argued that the diagram says more about the nature of meaning than about how the mind may or may not actually work. As a result, the diagram should be regarded as informing the necessary gradients related to the concept of logic that gives it meaning. All the concepts on the diagram are synonymous to the act of thought, and so it raises the question as to how the actual differences between these states of mind are constituted. The diagram demonstrates that logic is only one part of cognition. For example, in order to make sense of logic, all of the other concepts in the table above are required to render it meaningful. Like a hermeneutic circle where understanding the whole relies on the individual parts and vice versa. Such studies in hermeneutics by figures such as Dilthey (2010), Heidegger (2013) or Gadamer (1975) remain contentious as to whether this loop represents, logic, interpretation, ontology or a methodological problem. Consequently, it is not clear if these relations are particular to the mind or if the mind is particular to these relations. In other words, are these relations only to be found in the mind, or is the mind specifically tuned in to whatever is driving these relationships? These two seemingly contradictory questions are actually the same question, they point to contrast itself, an entity that cannot fully belong to either mind or that which is external to it. Therefore, in the process of questioning this, the line between interior and exterior deteriorates and the thinker has access to relationships usually off access to thought as thinking usually uses whatever is driving these relationships to think with.

*** 

The function of the fractal diagram presented above is to demonstrate visually how I have compiled the relationships between the concepts. However, the design of the diagram is somewhat linear in the way it demonstrates relationships, using straight horizontal, and vertical lines to represent the relationship between the concepts. This limits the extent to which it can be analogised to the relationships discovered around the concepts. The exercise above demonstrates that opposing concepts are not in a simple 2-dimensional scale and meaning cannot be imagined in this way or else meaning would become recessive. Therefore, the relationship shared between concepts in a spectrum must be graduated simultaneously away and back towards each other. This means that just as in the colour spectrum (or musical scales like the circle of fifths) a better way to represent the relationship would be as a wave or cyclically. This is not to assume (in the style of physicalism) that meaning is actually a wave or circle or has any physical presence but rather to relate meaning to what can be sensed and observed. The most readily observable spectrums are those of light and sound, which are understood as a wave with the variance of those waves resulting in variances of sight and hearing, sound and light can be used as a metaphor to similarly grade concepts across a wave of meaning.

To chart the diagram as a wave, the arrangement of the concepts cannot be in the same order in which they were first posed above. This is because the linear arrangement above would not gradate across the wave or form a replicating pattern. In order to form a pattern as a wave, the vertical lines need to take on the peaks of the wave and the horizontal lines take on the middle of the wave. Alternatively, the wave could be represented double-peaked as electromagnetic radiation often is. But for clarity, I will represent the set in one wave. (Therefore, the arrangement of concepts into a gradated, replicating pattern would rearrange positions in the fractal diagram order above to 1,3,2,4,5,7,6,8,9,11,10,12). Below the concepts have been arranged in a continuous concept spectrum wave:

**Figure I-3**

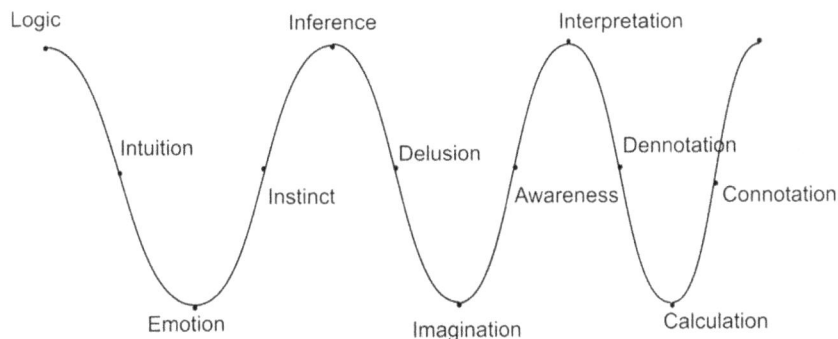

The frequency of the wave goes from high to low to give each concept its own wavelength. To better represent the relationship between opposing and related meanings, the wavelengths are represented as proportional to one another. Again, this is not to assume that meaning has a physical presence but to consider the ways in which it can be analogised to observable spectrums. Once charted, the wave can then be easily be transferred into a spectrum wheel:

**Figure I-4**

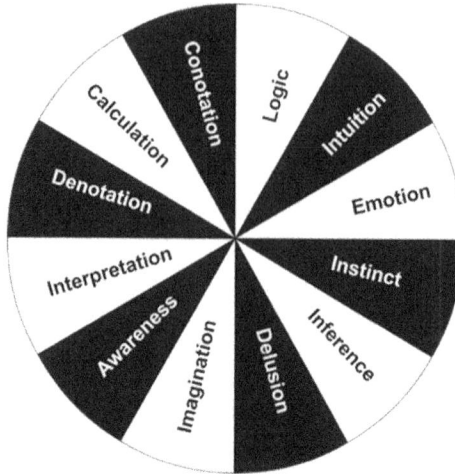

This diagram follows the order of the wave diagram. However, on the wave diagram above logic could be considered two have two places, one between connotation and intuition and another between denotation and connotation (and the same could be said of the fractal diagram, where the 4th, 8th and 12th position seem to float). This means that when each diagram is transferred to a wheel the positions can be reverse populated to reveal that each spectrum has two possible orders (if the first order is 1,3,2,4,5,7,6,8,9,11,10,12 the reverse order is 1, 12,2,3,5,4,6,7,9,8,10, 11). Demonstrated below:

**Figure I-5**

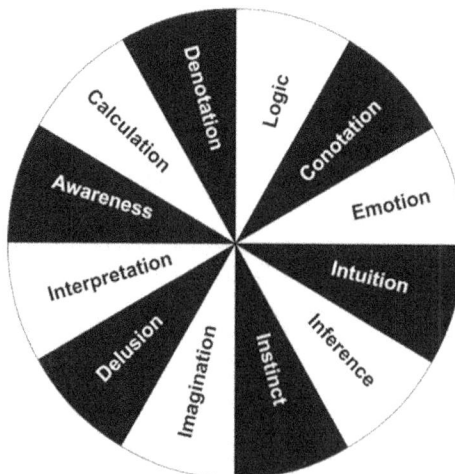

This means that every opposition has 2 'middle' concepts, but that all oppositional meanings remain the same. The reason for their being two orders is because these diagrams demonstrate that meaning is not linear, or binary. Rather they are an attempt to represent something which is infinite and so does not line up to a finite representation exactly. This can be imagined like the colour spectrum or the harmonic series, which also has no perfect arrangement in non-infinite systems.[13] Therefore, I do not wish to imply that meanings have any fixed boundary between each other. Rather, a concept sits among a range of other concepts that define what it means and its interdependent relationship. In the subsequent diagrams that follow, I will only compile the first order of the method into a spectrum wheel in the interests of concision.

***

Charting concepts in a wheel makes more visible further possible relationships shared between the concepts. For instance, the concepts across the wheel form some kind of complementary relationship (these are between positions 1 and 7; 2 and 8; 3 and 9; 4 and 10; 5 and 11; 6 and 12 in the fractal diagram). In this case, the complementary concepts are a simile of each other. The complementary relationships in this concept spectrum are: logic and Imagination; Intuition and awareness; emotion and interpretation; Instinct and literal thinking; deduction and calculation; delusion and connotation. Another relationship that can be explored is that two subsets of concepts can be formed by taking concepts spaced one across from each other (on the fractal diagram the first subset would be the 1st, 3rd, 5th, 7th, 9th and 11th positions, and the second subset would be the 2nd, 4th, 6th, 8th, 10th and 12th positions). For example, the first set of this spectrum would be: Logic; emotion; deduction; imagination; interpretation and calculation, and the second set would be intuition; instinct; delusion; awareness; literality and connotation. The relationship shared between these subsets is open to some interpretation, and it is unclear if they add any further meaning. I have highlighted these sets have been highlighted as they represent constants. For example, the oppositions, complementary relationships, the two subsets remain the same between both orders of the spectrum.

These patterns can then be used to validate the spectrum.

# Validating a Concept Spectrum

**Table I-1**

Below are summarised some of the key features of the diagram, they can be used to validate that the graph is correct, as well as be used for reference:

- The concepts must all be related to each other
- No repetitions of any of the concepts should occur
- The 1st and 7th; 2nd and 8th; 3rd and 9th; 4th and 10th; 5th and 11th; 6th and 12th positions on the fractal diagram should be complementary*
- The 1st, 3rd, 5th, 7th, 9th and 11th positions on the fractal diagram form a subset, as do the 2nd, 4th, 6th, 8th, 10th and 12th positions
- The concepts should gradate around the wave or wheel (this gradation has two orders when taken from the fractal diagram to the wheel 1,3,2,4,5,7,6,8,9,11,10,12 and 1,12,2,3,5,4,6,7,9,8,10,11)
- The cycle has 12 distinct, but related concepts that form a set

*Note that the concepts on a diagram should not be ranked, this numbering is done only with the intention of clarity.

The diagram that has been created is not limited to the concept of logic. The process used here can be used to plot other concepts, and the rest of the book will be dedicated to exploring further concepts that exemplify the method and what it implies for thought and meaning. But before continuing, the method so far described poses some challenges to the orthodoxy. Therefore, I will provide an initial summary with the aim of clarifying some of the implications of the method if accepted as valid:

- Each stage of the process is highly interpretive and throughout the process the contrasts between concepts need to be tested and retested until they begin to fit together as a whole. The resulting model relies upon the accuracy of the words used to represent each concept. However, as words carry connotation, the choice of words selected are liable to distort the concepts. This emphasises the importance of testing the diagram, as the relationship between the concepts can be understood as independent from the words of the diagram.

- Words carry connotation and their meanings may shift, but the symmetrical pattern from which words derive implies a meaning which informs the words. However, rather than imply that meanings are pre-determined, meaning is understood to be infinite and so not explicit until specifically assigned to words and language.

- Meaning has some flexibility between how it is expressed according to grammar or morphology, the grammar emerges as a result of consistent usage.

- Meanings change over time as they are highly interdependent, and a difference in initial concept will change the subsequent concepts on the diagram. Meanings can also shift across concepts through connotation. Only the most basic and common concepts can be isolated but even then, still carry connotation once they begin to be interpreted.

- Meaning itself should not be considered to be exhaustive. For example, concepts can be combined infinitely amongst themselves to have no limit of nuance. The spectrums detailed here are merely the regulation of meaning into equal positions. To be speculated is the extent to which meanings can be mixed between each other, and if the mixing of meanings follows some pattern like the mixing of colours.

- No position on the diagram should be considered as supreme, but as informed by the placement decreed by the previous meaning. Therefore, no meaning can be considered as absolute in isolation, but as the product of the relationship between the other positions on the diagram.

- No concept exists only as a dualism, so right and wrong; positive and negative etc. all have several other concepts that confound their relationship.

- Each of the concepts in the diagram can be understood as impartial and partial at the same time. For example, each concept meaning can be seen to derive from a regulated and repeatable rule or principle. However, they are also partial because each concept only represents one part of something bigger where an overarching meaning between all of the concepts on any diagram is not possible.

Also worth bearing in mind are some possible caveats and limitations to the method:

- The full significance of the pattern discovered is unknown. Could thought be possible with longer or shorter concept spectrums? I.e. if human though can divide a meaning 12 times might meaningful thought be possible that can divide concepts into, for example, 60 different, relatable concepts and therefore have a more nuanced intelligence than our own? It could be speculated here that the number of meanings could be related to the architecture of neurons sensing electromagnetic and chemical signals. Just as the sensation of colour is dependent on the number of cones in the eye, and discrepancies in cones alters the extent of discrepancy between colour hues. Perhaps different neural architecture accesses more nuance in meaning. Although it should be mentioned that in light of the evidence available such speculations are highly conjectural without more investigation.

- Can one concept appear to have the same meaning on one spectrum as it does on another? In order for the method as hypothesised here to be definitive, it must be assumed that specific meanings are exclusive to the spectrums where they occur. However, as the words used to convey meaning contain connotation and may not be accurate, some words may be very similar and may be difficult to judge independently to assess their exact differences. Testing that includes other people may help to affirm the best choice of words, however, no once and for all set of word relations can ever be compiled as language is imperfect and finite unlike meaning.

- The validity of the method and the results are difficult to assess with ulterior methods. As the method attempt to uncover the dynamics of meaning itself, to falsify such an idea would require a point of view positioned in meaninglessness.

- Compiling a spectrum becomes more difficult with concepts that are rhetorically convoluted with controversial meanings, or concepts where meanings are contentious. For example, communism v capitalism, science v magic. Concepts such as these are too contested to find their middle.

- Compiling a spectrum is also difficult when concepts are newly posited and discovered. For example, the contrasts posed in contemporary philosophical debate or scientific discovery.[14]

With these considerations in mind, the next chapter will use the method to speculate further on what it may imply for meaning and how sense may be derived from this pattern.

## Endnotes

[1] My approach to methods may also be broadly compared to hermeneutics with all of the benefits and limitations entailed by such methods. See for example Ricœur (1990a, 2003), who argues that language is generative/regenerative in the same way as metaphor, i.e. metaphorical meaning can be stated in novel ways and, as a consequence, language can be seen as containing within itself resources that allow it to be used creatively and non-exhaustively. The obvious limit of such a method is that it mediates and negotiates rather than remove the conflict of different interpretations (Makkreel, 2015). This means that answers may be made more complex rather than less and has an implication for the focus and detail of the research. My aim is not to argue that my approach to method is the only way to pursue truth or validity, but rather demonstrates a particular kind of validity.

[2] Parallels could be drawn between this tactic and long standing traditions in philosophy on the ease of creating new meaning with the simple opposition, see Heller-Roazen (2017).

[3] This is not to re-trod the debate between Putnam and Davidson (Putnam, 1975) as to whether meanings are contained in words or require sentences as here meaning is infinite and continuous where meanings can be formed and modified over all scales of language.

[4] This accounts for the break between sign and signifier of 20thC semiotics, or in semantics this was found out when attempting to set up a field of semantic differentials initiated by Osgood (1964). Osgood attempted to create a tool to identify the ways in which human cognition processes difference. The tool attempted to devise a set of universal antonyms that could represented the act of interpretation at its most broad and rudimentary that all subsequent words could be related back to. To test it they devised a huge cross-cultural cross language study, only to discover that many words were not considered similar to have similar values. This method can also be linked to machine learning, specifically the technique of word embedding.

[5] A founding principle of semiotics that has endured since Saussure is that meaning must always be generated in contrast to something else. "Each of a set of synonyms like redouter ('to dread'), craindre ('to fear'), avoir peur ('to be afraid') has its particular value only because they stand in contrast with one another. No word has a value that can be identified independently of what else is in its vicinity (Saussure)".

[6] Connotation, hermeneutics, baudrillard and relation. Baudrillard emphasises that any concept gets its meaning through a process of othering something else. But in this process meaning becomes self-referential and the internal relations between meanings do not point to anything external beyond themselves. There is some truth in this statement in that a self-referential process must be going on between meanings. However, if the meaning of a concept can be traced through a spectrum (or wave) it is

possible to understand a concept more precisely, and we also become aware of the other direct meanings that are affected. And harder for the meaning of something to shift as the meaning becomes triangulated against others.

[7] This makes it impossible to create a mathematical principle for the formula, as it is a process of finding meaning beyond logic.

[8] This most obviously points to dialectic as attributed to Hegel of thesis, antithesis and synthesis. However, some dispute exists between those interpretations attributed to Hegel and what Hegel's original conception was, as it has been argued that Hegel meant dialectic to determine that which was rational from that which was not, which is the opposite of what we are trying to do here.

[9] Instinct is notoriously difficult to define and the inclusion of this concept should no way imply that there exists a universal human instinct that is invariable. Within this diagram instinct is wholly dependent on all of the other concepts, and so in no way can it be seen as independent of logic or emotion, which are changeable.

[10] This concept has a much more extensive history. For example: Charles Sanderson Pierce broke inference down further into deduction, induction and abduction, that could be followed further (Peirce, 1878).

[11] The concepts of connotation and denotation may be compared to the analytical concepts of intension and extension proposed by Frege and developed in analytic philosophy by Carnap and Quine amongst others. Despite being made distinct by these accounts from the concept of connotation/denotation, there is still a similarity in the ways these concepts attempt to distinguish between meanings that are internal, and other things that are empirically "out there".

[12] No exactitude can currently be given as to why the method becomes recursive after 12 iterations or if it is possible to make a set of concepts using different numbers, other than it's a manageable number from which to organise concepts dialectically. For example, from the results of the method meanings can be broken down into smaller numbers of recursive words. The larger question would be if a further method could be devised to make larger or smaller groups. The nature of such a pattern is difficult to validate as one cannot step outside of meaning to do so. It can only be speculated as to whether there is something particular about sense to the number 12 given its greater factorability and hence divisibility (see the Dozenal Society of America www.dozenal.org and the Dozenal Society of Great Britain www.dozenalsociety.org.uk and mathematicians such as Alexander Aitkenor), or if this number is merely coincidental or the result of some other oversight. I wish to avoid posing the number 12 non-sceptically as anything more or less than the number already presented to us mathematically.

[13] For some, the capacity to comprehend the concept of infinity is a key characteristics of mind and consciousness, see Lucas (1961) and Penrose (1995). In a similar vein, Bernstein (1990) likens minds ability to appreciation music to its ability to acquire language.

[14] This is not to exclude the possibility that the method postulated gives a premise to review dense disciplinary terminologies on the grounds that if concepts struggle for opposition their meanings are less sustainable.

Chapter II

# Sense

To explore the relationship between dialectic and rhetoric further, the investigation should be expanded. Both dialectic and rhetoric can be seen as a means to free logic from emotion. Therefore, to proceed this enquiry emotion should be engaged in the same way as has been done for logic. Establishing logic from emotion is significant as it engages with some long-standing philosophical dualisms, most notably that of realism v idealism (present from Aristotle v Plato all the way up to the modern epoch), or more specifically, the attempt to understand the world free of our interpretation of it. In this section, I aim to contribute to this debate by opening out the question of what it is to make sense. Rather than limiting this investigation to one concept alone, using the method, I will extend these enquiries to the concepts that sense is foundered upon (such as logic, rationality, truth and the absolute) or attempts to exclude (in the case of emotion).

## Emotion

The idea of charting emotions as varying in smooth gradation across a continuum is as intriguing as it is worrying. As on the one hand, if such an undertaking were possible, it would give an insight on the experience of thinking and feeling as never before and help to link the human condition to patterns of nature observed around us (in observations such as the electromagnetic spectrum). But the worrying aspect on the other is what such an understanding of emotion would imply. For example, the capability to chart emotion with perfect accuracy would contrast with an individual's ability to express their own emotion as unique. An individual's reactions would no longer be their own and instead become an equation that can be worked out independently from the individual. As a result, endeavours to study emotion are chequered. Many ontological and epistemic definitions of emotions have been posed across a range of scientific disciplines. Yet to be resolved though, is how emotion can be resolved with perspectives that emphasise a discord between interpretation, or so-called phenomena and noumena independent of interpretation. On the one hand, if emotion is seen as a distinct and objective entity as in naturalism, perspectives struggle to define the purpose of emotion other than as a means for survival. Or at the other extreme, if emotion is to be understood as irreducible to any interpretation such as in affect theory (initiated by Tomkins, 1992), perspectives of emotion find it hard to define the line between where logic ends and emotion begins, leading to emotion and logic being seen as tantamount to the same thing or seeing logic as determined entirely by emotion. Such misperceptions mean that sciences, social sciences and humanities which may otherwise see emotion as elementary to the process of making sense, instead struggle to reliably establish what emotions are and are responsible for. Using the method devised, I will chart the contrast between the two in order to assert the distinction more fully.

So far, the model of logic above has emphasised that emotion is opposed to logic and related it to 11 other contrasting concepts of cognition. Relating emotion to cognition raises the question of at which point conscious thought and the rest of our bodily sensations meet.[1] Emotion is imperative to our understandings of experience, and in no way detachable from the rest of thought in general (a point implicit to rhetoric, prevalent in the enlightenment due to Hume, 2008; but for which modernist thinking has been repeatedly accused of ignoring see Horkheimer, 2002; or Simmel, 2015). In this interpretation however, it is not possible to define with certainty if conscious thoughts are an emotion or if emotions are conscious thoughts as both are integrally linked to each other. Which poses a problem as to which one has primacy over the other and where the other one goes when we are either feeling an emotion or thinking a thought. For example, if when reading this passage a reader may not consider themselves as detached from either thought or emotion, how can the information be communicated at all if not considered as in some way independent from the immediate emotion felt when reading it? Emotion and thought cannot be considered apart, yet without distinction and contrast are hard to define. In this way, emotion must add something crucial (or essential) to conscious thought. In the process of becoming familiar with something, information must be experienced with differing feelings and emotions as a way to know and understand that information in more depth (concurred by neuroscience Damasio, 2006; Berthoz, 2009). What is needed then is a method to conceptualise this contradiction where both the interrelation and the distinction of emotion is essential to the process of building both consciousness and knowledge.

Philosophy has traditionally found it difficult to consolidate thought and emotion, and such enquiries are where philosophy and science meld (most obviously seen in empiricism). Some like Goffman (1968) would portray emotions as emanating from a subject's interactions with the outside world, while others like Darwin (1872) would see emotion as emanating from instinct or biology. In between the two are a wide range of approaches such as Heidegger (2013) or James (2011) that pose that thought, emotions and the senses in general are processes of the same thing. Of contention to all such accounts is the contradiction involved when representing logic or emotion as independent whilst also interdependent, e.g. where can the subject be seen to exist amongst a system of discordant agencies? As a result, accounts such as these struggle to demonstrate how emotions are part of a larger process whilst also being distinct opposing entities. These accounts invariably must choose between emphasising the primacy of either thought, emotion, the senses, the outside world, or all of these aspects as an interdependent holistic system.

This discordance is made more pronounced when considering basic or core emotions. Basic emotions are said to be a set of emotions that are universal and that all emotions can be broken down into. Many prominent figures such as Descartes, Plato and Darwin have posed lists of varying lengths as to what can be considered to be the basic emotions. However, if emotions are strictly regimented and can be listed off yet interdependent to conscious thought, they must contrast the experience of conscious thought which is reflexive and can be altered and reprogrammed. Emotion can be more readily imagined as objective compared to consciousness which requires abstraction to be objective. What is needed, therefore, is a system that equilibrates thought with regulated emotions in an infinite system that allows conscious thought unlimited reflexivity. In other words, what is implied is a continuum or spectrum of emotion. Closest to this aim is the work of psychologists William McDougall, Harold Schlosberg and Robert Plutchik who have compiled a circumplex of basic emotions. Their work compares emotion to colour and then sets about mapping emotions to a colour spectrum to compile a circumplex model of emotion:

**Figure II-1** Plutchik's (2001) Circumplex of Emotions

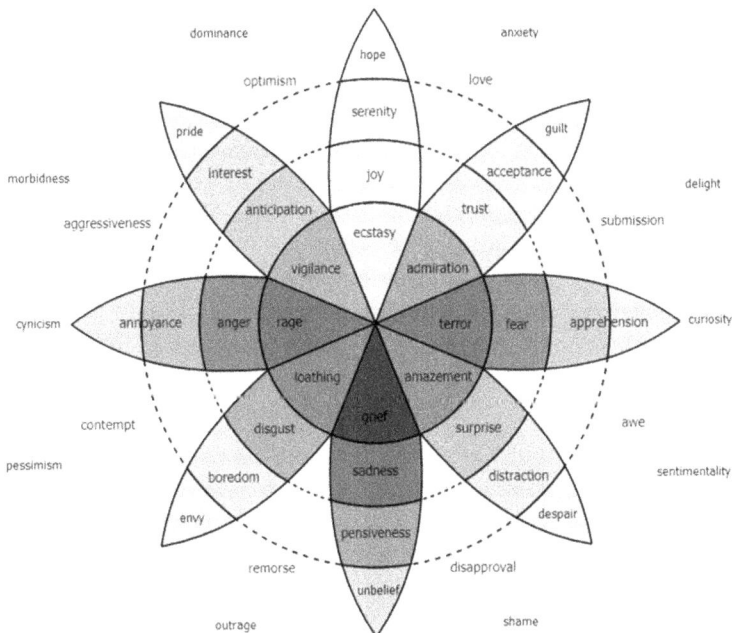

Plutchik's (2001) (derived from McDougall, 1909, chap. 2) model puts emotions together into a circumplex which expands outward to account for the intensity of the emotion. The model organises emotion into opposing categories that emphasise the extent to which the emotions are interrelated. This makes it much more sophisticated than accounts offering a list alone. Strictly speaking however, the circumplex compiled is not a spectrum as it is not in a continuum. Rather than being contained on the wheel, the emotions extend outwards. Therefore, the emotions are presented in intersecting axis, but have no real verification as to how they progress around the wheel and are not self-referential. If emotions are understood as a circumplex it becomes difficult to understand the relation between emotion and other cognition processes, as emotions must change thoughts and vice versa. A circumplex would imply an unaccountable extra dimension to emotion going outwards in a linear fashion, making it harder to understand how emotion and cognition are linked in a continuous causal system. A circumplex model therefore, makes it difficult to understand emotion as a thought.

As an alternative, I will use the experimental method outlined in the previous chapter to render emotion as it is conceptualised. This is not in an attempt to render emotion as it is felt, but rather dynamics of making them meaningful as the experience of emotion must always have something that escapes the concept and vice versa. This underlines the usefulness of a spectrum however, in that a spectrum implies that emotions are infinite and boundless, whilst also comprehensive when in their specific forms. As can be compared with spectrums of colour or musical notes the number of possible hues or pitches is overwhelmingly extensive, yet the number of colours or notes given more extensive definition fits about 7 or 12. The concept of an emotion and the sensation of an emotion are interdependently linked (Serres, 2008). But a concept is limited in ways in which an emotion is not. The number of possible meanings is probably infinite, but in order to make a concept comprehendible, it must be ordered into a more manageable set of interrelating concepts in order for it to gain meaning. The mystery here is to consider why something potentially infinite should imply fixed and finite relations, however as a mystery, it is one we more or less take for granted in meaningful communication. Therefore, to create a spectrum of emotions, the spectrum should be made of concepts spaced in symmetrical intervals that reflect the ways in which emotions are also opposed to each other.

Rather than create a list arbitrarily therefore, analysis will begin with the concept of one emotion and use it as the basis from which to derive the others. In this case, this will be ecstasy, but theoretically, the whole wheel could be derived from any of the other emotions that will be found using ecstasy:

**Figure II-2**

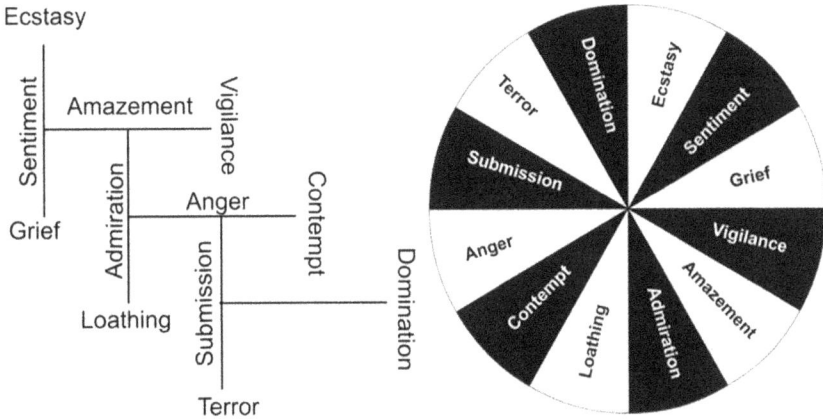

**Table II-1**

| Ecstasy | Amazement | Rage |
|---|---|---|
| Plutchik understands ecstasy as the feeling derived from gaining something deemed as valuable.<br><br>Grief<br><br>Grief is therefore the opposite of ecstasy as it is the feeling of losing something valuable.<br><br>Sentiment<br><br>In between ecstasy and grief is the feeling of both happiness and sadness, which can be understood as sentiment.<br><br>Vigilance<br><br>The feeling of vigilance is the opposite of sentiment as it is the feeling needed to explore something and therefore reserving feeling until a cognitive judgement can be made. | Between sentiment and vigilance is the feeling of amazement, which serves as the feeling held when a discovery has been made.<br><br>Loathing<br><br>The opposite of amazement is loathing which is the feeling of disgust, boredom or annoyance with something which inhibits wanting prolonged contact with that thing.<br><br>Admiration<br><br>Admiration is between amazement and loathing and is the feeling of accepting or including something.<br><br>Contempt<br><br>Contempt is the opposite of admiration and is the feeling of wishing to challenge, deride or ridicule something. | Rage is between admiration and contempt as it is the feeling of being admiring and contemptuous at the same time in the way in which one may be towards an enemy.<br><br>Terror<br><br>Terror is the opposite of rage and activates the impulse to not fight but to flee.<br><br>Submission<br><br>Submission is between terror and rage and is the feeling of accepting something which you would otherwise avoid.<br><br>Domination<br><br>Domination is the opposite of submission and is the feeling of complete power and confidence over something, which leads us back to the concept of ecstasy. |

The validity of each concept on the wheel can be assessed by looking at the complimentary relationship with the concept on the opposite side of the wheel. In this case, the complimentary relationship forms an alternate contrasting concept. The wheel also forms two 'odd' and 'even' sets spaced at one segment removed around the wheel. Ecstasy; grief; amazement; loathing; rage and terror could be termed as 'feeling' emotions that promote inner feeling over thought. Sentiment; vigilance; admiration; contempt; submission and domination could be seen as 'thinking' emotions that promote thinking over inner feeling.

The results above differ from the studies of emotion discussed that attempt to compare emotion to an observable external independent event, what is more readily demonstrated here is the conceptual interrelations between the emotions themselves. The table above does not claim to provide a comprehensive mechanism for how emotion functions, or an exhaustive depiction of all possible emotions (such an endeavour may be impossible to ever fully verify). Rather this spectrum represents how concepts of emotion can be arranged into a self-contained system. Caution must also be expressed as to whether this affirms Darwin's (2018) assertion that emotions are universal, as the concepts found are in the English language and culture. Any inferences made from the table above rely entirely on the extent of the likeness between concept and emotion. If emotion is imagined as calibrated to thought, it must work along similar translational principles. Without the mind, matter has no expression, without matter the mind has no function. Therefore, through emotions mind meets matter, emotion is the necessary contrast that links thought to feeling and feeling to the wider world. Emotion and consciousness are designed to work inter-dependently (as widely explored in the concept of psyche). The more an emotion is not trusted, the more it becomes undeniable, conversely the more we trust only our emotions the less we understand them. Consciousness and emotion are therefore independent, but however we may wish to theorise emotion, there is no real option to think reflexively detached from or contrary to emotion.

Emotion's great paradox is that it presents to logic and consciousness in the same way as does an external object, yet at the same time emotion also greatly informs the sense of meaning and selfhood. Of the other concepts on the table of logic presented above, emotion is the only concept so readily undeniable to the individual. As a result, an individual's experience of emotion is deeply entwined with their sense of nature, as emotion presents itself as a personal nature deeply embedded in the individual yet also just beyond reach. When explored with the method presented above, emotion renders the dualism of subject and object non-exclusive; emotion transcends both (and by extension, other dualisms such as thought and experience; the individual and reality). In order to continue to explore these dualisms further, the book will proceed by using the method to continue to enquire about how this understanding of meaning relates to knowledge of the world, starting with rationality.

## Rationality

Emotion and logic have been described above as integrally linked to the point where they are interdependent with neither one holding primacy over the other. In this schema, logic is the process that comprehends and makes emotion intelligible, and emotion is that which authenticates logic and determines its value and importance.[2] The relationship between logic and emotion is further complimented by the concepts discovered in the first spectrum above. Presenting logic and emotion in an interdependent relationship opens up to question how senses, feelings and ideas combine or contrast and how some thoughts stand out as more prescient or persuasive than others? This brings into focus the concept of rationality or reason, as reason is taken to mean an adjudication of whether a logic or emotion are 'reasonable' or not. This corroborates the grand traditions of Western philosophy which have found it difficult to separate logic and reason from the concept of logos (see Stambovsky, 1996). Consequently, using the concept of rationality or reason with the method compiled is of interest here, and may help to further understand the dynamic relationships between the subject, the senses and the wider world around them.

Reason was a foundational concept to the enlightenment of the 17th and 18th centuries and was encouraged as an accompaniment to not only science but governance of almost all facets of human endeavour. However, with the rise of the idealisms of the 19th century the concept of reason became more extreme, epitomised in Hegel's (1967) summation that "the rational alone is real", which presented reason as an all-encompassing force of nature. This understanding of reason was backlashed against in the late 19th and early 20th centuries by movements identifying with analytical or empiricalEmpiricism approaches (e.g. analytical philosophy and logical positivism). By the second half of the 20th century, the dangers of such a position on reason became apparent when accompanied by political and historical atrocities on scales unimaginable, and as a result, disillusionment grew with the concept of rationality (Arendt, 1951; Bauman, 1991; Jankélévitch, 2013). In the time since, the greater part of the human sciences across virtually all epistemological divides have held major reservations towards the concept of reason (Arnett, 2012). The biggest concern has been with the implicit duplicity associated with 'reasonable' concepts such as progress, or universality, or so-called grand narratives. Most notably, by which standard are we to judge or founder the reasonability of their claim? No such all-encompassing value exists without exception. This raises a concept of reason that is all the more problematic but tricky to deny as any attempt to critique reason must itself form an alternate reason, which then in itself becomes a new reason (Laruelle, 2017a). Applying the method devised should therefore give a better understanding of what concepts reason is related to and offer a countenance. Such a move will allow reason to be more directly linked to logic and emotions:

**Figure II-3**

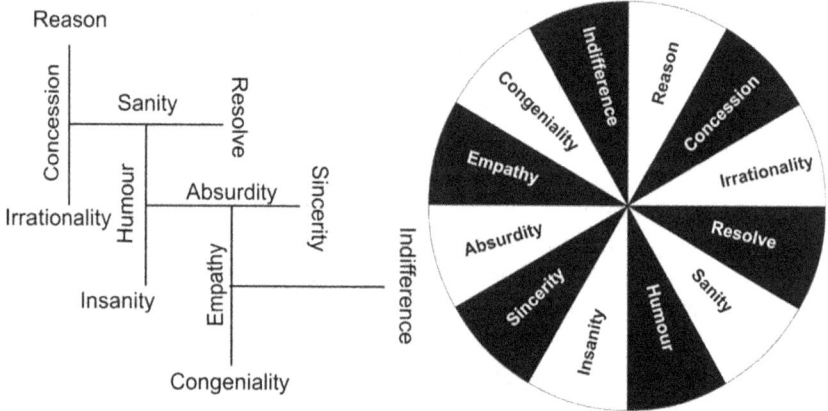

**Table II-2**

| Reason | Insanity | Congenial |
|---|---|---|
| A reason is to assume the degree something may make sense, or is rational. | The opposite of even-minded is insanity (which is cautiously highlighted as this meaning may have some consequence). | The opposite of absurdity is the sense of something being convivial. This is something humorous that doesn't need to be taken seriously. |
| Irrationality | Humour | Sympathy/empathy |
| The opposite of that is the concept whereby a thought process does not make sense which is irrationality. This concept could also be described as a feeling or belief that is vague or irrational. | The middle between sanity and insanity is the humour of not being sure the line between the two. | Lying between a sense of absurdity and congeniality is a sympathy or empathy, as seeing someone experiencing absurdity or congenialities evokes a sympathy if one is seeking to understand either of them. |
| Concession | Seriousness | |
| Between reason and irrationality is concession as | The opposite of amusement is take a thought seriously. | |

| when reason or irrationality meet, either one has to make a concession if it is to reconcile with the other in any way.<br><br>Resolve<br><br>The opposite of making a concession is to be resolute and make no concession<br><br>Sanity<br><br>Between conceding and being resolute is the concept of being equable to both, which I have cautiously termed as sanity. | Absurdity<br><br>Between amusement and seriousness is absurdity. This is the sense that something is profoundly funny yet having no chance not to take it seriously. | Detachment<br><br>The opposite of sympathy is a psychological detachment which chooses not to see the plight of others sympathetically. This brings the wheel back to rationality as that which is rational is the ability to respond with sympathy but detachment, reason is the individual seeking to make sense of the world beyond their immediate reaction to it. |
|---|---|---|

The complimentary relationship opposes the concepts on the other side. The odd/even relationship; reason; irrationality; sanity; insanity; tediousness and boredom are all inward states of the mind. Concession; resolve; humour; sincerity; empathy and indifference are all outward dispositions of the character or personality.

Using the experimental method offers a more nuanced understanding of the concept of reason. The table implies reason to be performative rather than innate. The placement of reason in the table gives it no precedent over any of the other finely balanced highly interdependent concepts it relates to. Reason as presented here is finely poised amongst the other concepts that relate to its meaning, and so no one reason can ever be said to be a reason regardless of the other concepts it relates to. Rather than descending into relativism, the other concepts in the table demonstrate that reason is entwined with the understanding of a whole range of dispositions such as what is amusing, or what should be taken as serious. The concept of reason therefore, is linked with its ability to be reflexive of both logical and emotional states, and is as inwardly facing as it is outwards. This initiates the question of where the rationale to reflect on these concepts can be located. More specifically, when considering the results above, the spectrum's own rationality becomes confused. The steps taken to compile the table pose no threat to reason, and neither do the relationships once completed. Rather it is the conclusion that the spectrum is to be held as credible whilst demonstrating the necessary limits of reason that conflicts with the rationale. It implies the discovery of a universal rationale that cannot possibly be universal. To demonstrate reason as above therefore, relies upon an understanding of reason as limited and specified. Here reason is more akin to a sense that is intrinsically engaged with the contrast between concepts and their opposite. Such an assertion makes the independent apeiron that seems to initiate the sense all the more enigmatic. So far, many concepts have been demonstrated as linked to sense such as logic, emotion, impulse, reason etc. Rather than offering a definitive explanation of contrast, however, each concept seems to initiate another.

This does not fit neatly into the received wisdom of idealism or empiricism on reason. In the longstanding view of Kant 'knowledge begins with the senses, proceeds then to understanding and ends with reason', which is developed to mean that any observation deriving from sense can never do so independent of its own interpretation (Kant, 2007). Kant's proof for this derives from antinomy. For Kant, antinomy – or contradiction – demonstrates some sort of extra ability to reason, and provide proof as to how ideals are transcendent beyond what can be known empirically. My own account of sense does not wish to deny transcendence entirely, but rather nuance our understanding of it by posing contrast as pre-eminent to reason. I argue that contradiction is merely a form of contrast and that contrast is a prerequisite to both thought and the assertion of an objects and physicality. For example, how could one demonstrate a sensation without the contrast with which to differentiate it. Contrast cannot be wholly transcendent as it is the very substance of sensation, yet it is also impossible to quantify as it is the very point of transition between sense and that which is sensed. As such, if reason is transcendental so too would be physical objects as they are both forged and only ever found in the contrast between other things. The existence of a gradated spectrum of concepts that repeats after 12 iterations seems to demonstrate that reason and meaning are as observable as any other object, and so denies the physical from occupying a realm aside from reason, and so reason is in some way irrevocably linked to other physical forces.

This point is similar to Hegel's (1967) own criticism of Kant (and the position of absolute idealism in general), which argues that reason itself is something that exists independently of its observer (also similar to Schopenhauer's, 1819 own objection that 'we can know the thing-in-itself because we are it'). Hegel's take on antinomy is that it is actually evidence of 'a unity of opposites'; where finite concepts are only knowable once made infinite by their opposing concept, and so are different aspects of the same thing.[3] However, Hegel also did not consider contrast, for him reason was not derived from sense but was itself a direct manifestation of the apeiron behind oppositions. To understand reason through the unity of opposites is to argue that reason will become more and more aware of itself unto absolution. Hegel's stance on idealism understands reason as underived and not determined by anything else.[4] Such a view of reason overexerts the value of reason at the expense of other concepts which may contrast it. To avoid this, the method used here offers a way to demonstrate how both reason and the objects which reasons observe are made distinct through contrast. Contrast always offers an exception or some margin of error by highlighting the point between concepts beyond any one unity.

Therefore, the results of the method can be said to demonstrate a pattern evidencing some sort of meaning independent to the thinker, yet what is evidenced is impossible to be represented consistently with words. This puts the method in a juxtaposition to both Kant and Hegel, i.e. displaying an absolute meaning that cannot be reflected absolutely with meaning (not dissimilar to Meillassoux, 2009). The method postulated is an attempt to maintain a position that avoids serving one position over and above another, rather it attempts to remain in the contrast between conceptions. Rather than render my position as lacking definition or meaning, this is precisely the point of meaning. All concepts must be self-validating and recursive otherwise they could not be referred back to themselves and rendered meaningful. Concepts become more idealistic when pursued to an extreme (Foucault demonstrates this profoundly when arguing that the only opposite that our civilisation knows to reason is madness). The table above demonstrates that reason may be transformed in a different situation or may be overridden. For example, reason must be just as applicable to emotion and to other sensations as it is to logic, and the reason for emotions and other sensations may at times be more prescient than logical ones. Alongside logic and emotion, reason should also be seen as gaining meaning through contrast. Both emotion and logic have their own relationship to reason, and the reason for one may contradict the other whilst both still being reasonable.

This point could be said to be close to dialetheism - which, depending on your stance, states that some or all contradictions are true (such as presented by Priest, 2006b on contradiction). However, here I wish to propose a key difference, when concepts are related together into bivalent propositions they cease to be authentic, untainted versions of themselves and gain the connotations of bivalence. Therefore, bivalent sentences articulate towards the truths or fallacies of concepts that they can never fully encapsulate the full meaning of. Truths (as much as we can imply them) can only ever be found in the concept of truth itself which is tainted when formed into a specific sentence (see Estrada-Gonzalez, 2012 who argues the impossibility of demonstration all possible truth values with logic alone). There is no way to transmit meaning without using a tense, clause or sentence as there is no way to join up concepts into coherent logical arguments. Therefore, sentences can be believed to be more or less truthful, or even dialethic, but never fully articulate one consistent logic alone that will always be true. This could be said to represent a paraconsistent logic (in the words of Priest, 2006b) - that a contradiction can be more or less true in certain circumstances. However, I wish to question if such inconsistent logic should be called a logic at all? Is there no limit to the extent to which logic can be stretched? If the understanding of logic relies on an understanding of what logic is not, all things knowable cannot be considered to be exclusively logical. The tables above demonstrate a consistency in meaning that cannot be reduced to any one concept alone (such as the concept of logic). This implies that meaning encompasses logic and reason, but also infinitely surpasses it. This way of understanding meaning therefore demonstrates authentic experience beyond language (as analytical philosophy tends to avoid). This demonstrates an important distinction between the experience of contradiction which is logocentric and isolated to language and contrast for which is beyond language and non-logocentric (and so as with Meillassoux's 2012 criticism of dialectic, contradiction here should not be considered as necessary, not for the reason that we should understand reality as absolutely contingent however, but because the more we search for necessity or the absolute the more we find contrast).

To further demonstrate this point I will posit a non-standard interpretation of the principle of the identity of indiscernibles by Leibnitz; which states that there cannot be separate objects or entities that have all their properties in common. Logic must refer to things other than itself otherwise it is set on an infinite journey to distinguish indiscernibilities. Attempting to reflect on logic with logic results in more and more nuance not more logical logic (as demonstrated by Quine (1943), who for similar reasons thought modal logic impossible, but was later developed by Kripke (2015) as demonstrating logics ability to be both necessary and contingent). If logic is part of the world it reflects, it can never encompass the whole of it. Therefore, nothing other than actual reason can be considered reasonable, and as logic and reason can only ever be positioned in reflection, no one logic or reason can ever encompass all of the aspects of the being it is attempting to reflect at once, and any logic or reason is always only one part of the reality which provides the conditions for its existence. As a result, the emotions and sensations which reason reflects often experience the meaning of contrast more profoundly than the explanatory power of logic or reason can fully capture. Accordingly, logic and reason never have unlimited access to whatever they reflect, but at the same time never cease to be in some way similar to what is reflected (through contrast). Logic and reason must mediate with whatever opposes them. This means maintaining a contradiction between whatever reason and logic reflect and what logic and reason are when reflected upon, the discrepancies between the two constitutes the distinction of the finitude of logic from the infinity of meaning. Consequently, the limit of logic and reason is that they can only ever reflect upon meaning, whilst at the same time do nothing but represent one specific reality always to leave some further meaning aside.

Two concepts become important in light of the analysis of reason above; the absolute and truth. If logics, reasons and emotions are not inherently true and false what implications does this have for the things we see as absolute, or as truths? I will therefore turn to these two concepts next, starting with the absolute.

## The Absolute

The depiction of reason above has consequences for how the concept of the absolute is understood. If the contrast between concepts can be used to demonstrate an absolute limit of meaning, then what is this contrast? Contrast considered to be an infinite void would imply that within contrast resides nothing. This results in a negative existential paradox however (evocative of Meinong, 1960): as if nothing is considered as absolute, then something is absolute, nothing. If nothing is absolute, then nothing must encompass everything thereby not being nothing but everything. Contrast seems to imply both the descriptive and causal theories of reference, i.e. referring to something external whilst also only casually relative to referents (encompassing the Frege-Russell view with its opposition by Kripke, 2015). Or in Structuralist terms, contrast comprises both signifier and signified. The meaning of concepts resides in contrast which is infinitely suspended at the point between where sense meets that which is being sensed. Although concepts may not be describing the actual physical or material particles (as Putnam, 2012 demonstrates this would be implausible), the interiority or exteriority (or by extension the physics or ideal aspects) of contrast cannot be determined. What is being referenced implies a level of purity that is unachievable practically. As a result, our tenuous and ephemeral access to the absolute must be accepted, its meaning can be known whilst its totality cannot. This means that the concept of the absolute cannot escape the equal and opposite extreme; i.e. the concept of the relative. When making any statement or postulation (i.e. the act of relating words together), to imply something as absolute must be done in comparison to something relative, even if that absolute is to assert a relative uncertainty and vice versa.

The consequence of this is that the history of both philosophy and science can be read as a series of positions and counter-positions somewhere between the two. Both extreme absolutism or relativism are to be avoided in the fear that absolutism causes accounts to be dogmatic and ignore exceptions, while relativism renders language to lack definition and have no underlying consistent principles or rules to base itself in. As a result, the philosophical task could be interpreted as the search for an absolute that allows all exceptions, whilst not being too relative as to have no meaning at all (demonstrated by accounts such as Haraway, 1988). Philosophy is understandable as perpetuated by a careful balance of alignments and denouncements (see Laruelle, 2017b). The absolute therefore, is of prime interest to both dialectic and rhetoric as it perpetuates discussion. Even post-structural, post 'grand narrative' philosophies setting themselves the express task of disavowing absolutism have struggled to stray far from the absolute. Just as one such philosophy declares that there is no absolute along comes another philosopher to accuse that non-absolute of actually being an absolute. Throughout philosophy, the dialectical absolutes of one period turn into the rhetorical relativities of another. Therefore, in amongst such an array of philosophy, it could be argued that the only absolute ever successfully demonstrated has been philosophy's own ability to contradict itself. Therefore, the absolute forms the next curiosity to inform a concept spectrum:

**Figure II-4**

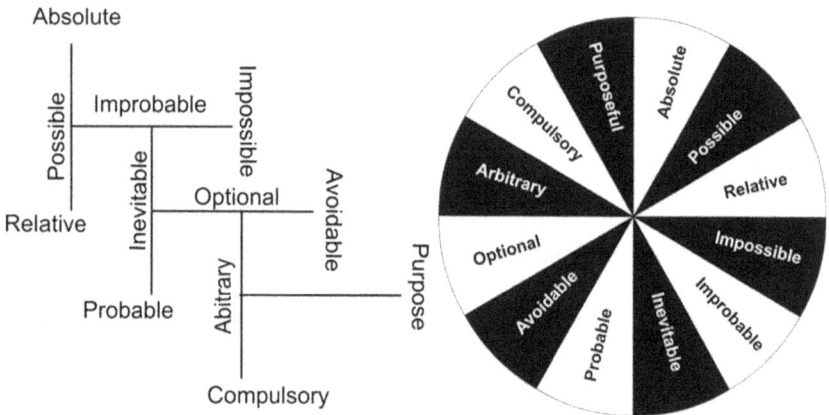

**Table II-3**

| Absolute | Improbable | Optional |
|---|---|---|
| If the absolute can be termed as that which is unchanging between deployments (the only thing fulfilling this criterion being nothing). | Between the possible and impossible is the improbable, something that is not impossible but also not very likely of possible to happen. | In between the inevitable and avoidable is the optional, the liberty to choose a foreseeable course of events. |
| **Relative** | **Probable** | **Compulsory** |
| The opposite of that which is unchanging would be that which may change in accordance with deployments. | The opposite of the improbable is something probable, something that is likely to happen. | The opposite of the optional is the compulsory, a foreseeable course of events where there is no choice but to comply. |

| Possible | Inevitable | Arbitrary |
|---|---|---|
| Between that which is absolute or relative is that which is possible as it is something that may be absolute or relative but can only be known once a certain deployment takes place.<br><br>Impossible<br><br>The opposite of something possible is something impossible, i.e. something that is not possible no matter the deployment. | In between the improbable and probable is the inevitable, something that is unavoidable to happen in the foreseeable future.<br><br>Avoidable<br><br>The opposite of the inevitable is the avoidable, something which can be prevented. | Between the optional and the compulsory is the arbitrary, which is where a choice is possible but made independently of the individual for which it affects.<br><br>Purpose<br><br>The opposite of the arbitrary is the purposeful where a choice is possible and has been planned in accordance with all aspects possible to foresee. Between the arbitrary and the purposeful is the absolute, which is both arbitrary and of purpose. |

The table highlights that the concept of the absolute is related to 11 other concepts that vary in their degree of absolution. None more interesting than the juncture between the absolute and purpose, intent or design. For those who seek absolute knowledge, the importance of purpose and design is of prime importance, as an absolute cannot be worked out independently of the purpose behind carrying out the task. For example, the grand goal of metaphysics (or physics) to seek the absoluteness of the universe, can only be known through knowing the purpose of the universe, and the only way to be able to know the absoluteness or purpose of the universe would be to be able to know the universe in its entirety without exception. Therefore, everything knowable to us as part of the universe must also be partial. As a result, the concepts on any of the spectrums done with the method presented can never be absolute, the concepts must be extremes that always remain a partial interpretation and never become fully achieved. This leads to a tantalising idea: that if concepts are only a part of something bigger, there must also be a 'something bigger' than ourselves. This 'something bigger' must be impossible to describe as a concept as the concepts make up only a part of it (which is demonstrated with Tarski's 1956 indefinability theorem). However, as all concepts are derived from this 'something bigger' they also cannot avoid reflecting and altering it in some way. This again echoes Hegel (this time with the Science of Logic) by implying a link between the absolute with reason, and reason with purpose. Reason and the absolute are being demonstrated here as related and self-fulfilling (i.e. ad-hominine). For example, the search for an absolute reason is the purpose behind the search for the absolute. Whenever this search picks a direction (e.g. looking for something bigger) another direction is inadvertently left behind (e.g. bigger or smaller, before or after, middle or extremity). Rather than understand this as reason's will for unity however, as Hegel does, the meaning here can be seen to be derived from a sense of the infinite between definite forms. No such pre-defined unity (opposition or contradiction) is implied, rather what is suggested is that the sense is residing in the middle of all things from a position of ultimate contrast and indeterminacy (rather than a unity this implies a parliament).

Testament to this is that every epoch of philosophy has struggled with the concept of the absolute, whether it be in the form of asserting a supreme being, state or a principle to founder thought. Yet ironically, it has remained possible to deny all such posed absolutes. Far from being a benign question, the historical attempts to establish absolutes has in equal measure from ancient to modern times been the cause of oppressions and wars as well as granting grand faiths and legitimisations. Greco-Roman inspired philosophy has been explicitly aware of these pitfalls and as a result (though not exclusive so) the search for the absolute has been tantamount to the search for either pure reason or infallible empiricism (as opposed to emotion. i.e. stoic), termed more broadly as the search for first principles. But even through its best efforts, (and those of the enlightenment or what has led up to the current era) neither philosophy nor science have been able to founder any singular one principle that links all other theories and observations together. Philosophy has long vied between its different epistemologies as how to reason 'what is bigger than us?' or 'what we are part of?' (and has led to an insurmountable succession of epistemes full of corners, caveats and meanders impossible to offer a succinct disposition of all of the philosophical positions posed). The most eminent dualism of which (with longstanding origins) has been between whether to look for the absolute empirically in the world around us, or only ever as an ideal of and in the mind.[5] Taken as a whole, this dualism seems to perpetuate exceptionality and indeterminacy.

The inheritance of this question into modern philosophy has accompanied the aims of science. Just as science has established its method to observe reality independent to perception. Philosophy has attempted to accompany this endeavour by testing this link between sense or experience and knowledge as a means to establish an 'actual' world separate to our perceptions of it. Manifesting differently in the analytic and continental traditions but has nevertheless been at the forefront of both (Braver, 2007). As these enquiries have developed the link between science and certain positions of the human sciences has become strenuous (reading between the lines of Labinger and Collins, 2001 about the "science wars" demonstrates this history). This is because philosophy has taken on the role of making compatible the social and cultural consequences of scientific advancement. This has developed through several stages that can be crudely put as from the empirical (asserting an unbroken link between the human subject and reality), to the phenomenological (understanding that the 'real world' may differ from the phenomena the human subject may receive in consciousness) and procedural (being unsure of both the real world and conscious phenomena beyond the processes which make either one comprehendible), in which time scientific method has stayed relatively unchanging. Recent developments of this philosophical enquiry found in Meillassoux (2009) decries that it is an absurdity to be sure that you are unsure of an independent reality, as it would result in you being sure of something even if it is an uncertain reality, thereby demonstrating that it is not possible to hold no position or belief on reality as such a position is still a position. This insight has led to a renewed belief in a reality independent to the observer breathing a new life into some hitherto heavily exhausted philosophical traditions. It has led to a whole movement in speculative realism that seeks access to a reality devoid of the thinker (see Brassier et al., 2007). Although authors under this umbrella have different opinions on how this reality is to be accessed (or even its overall coherence Wolfendale, 2019), the aspect of speculative realism that supposedly unites the trend is the description of a gap between the independent reality that can be deduced to exist whilst acknowledging the terrifying absence of ever knowing it with certainty. Despite the speed, momentum and best interests of this movement, it is still powerless to repeat the philosophical traditions before it (as Golumbia, 2016 demonstrates).

In a similar fashion the method used here cannot confirm anything to close this gap (because the focus here is the gap itself), but nor does it offer a condemnation of any grand philosophical or scientific traditions (and even the ones already discussed should not be viewed as superseded merely as having a contrast). The catalyst that my own inquiry is built upon is that the only means to access a constant is in contrast to something else. As analysis here is no longer on things in themselves, but on the contrast between, the numerous forms of idealism and empiricism are as compatible as they are incompatible to a perspective from contrast. Meaning can be understood simultaneously as a sense (ideal) whilst also being sensed (empirical). The meaning spectrums imply the existence of a pattern (emanating from a sense of contrast) that must be external as well as internal to meaning. The resulting range of concepts from the spectrum are always partial and indeterminate and therefore confirm and disaffirm all other concepts equally (and all grand philosophical traditions are equally confirmed and disaffirmed along with it). This has been maintained as a means to reason logic with emotion, as well as all our senses with whatever is in contrast to them. However, this puts us into a tricky relationship with the 'truth', which is explored in the next section.

# Truth

Reason is part of a range of concepts that refers to inner emotional, mental or sensory states towards exterior realities, the absolute seeks to validate a way of thinking in the face of uncertainty. The combination of the two demonstrates that no one concept alone in isolation can be considered entirely true. This produces a tricky position with truth, because if the concepts found by completing a spectrum are related, this represents a 'truth' in itself. Therefore, if the relationship is true, this would make it an absolute. Nietzsche (2003) notoriously challenges the relationship between truth and the absolute, concluding that absolute truth is impossible and instead truth relies upon different perspectives where no one perspective is definitively true. This premise has initiated a massive range of positions around the broad believe that philosophical thinking begins with the fallible human subject- not merely the thinking subject. The idea has undoubtedly had a profound impact not only on the governance and balance of long-established state and religious regimes, but also on subsequent thought right across the human sciences (De Man, 1996). Ideas such as 'post-truth' and 'perspectivism' have been developed and still have an unresolved and multifarious relevance to society and politics (including modern forms such as Gabriel, 2017). At the end of the 20[th]C, most faculties of the humanities and the social sciences conducting critical thought (e.g. critical theory or post-structuralism) in one way or another perpetuated perspectivism, which served as a challenge to the heirs of these schools in 21stC to overcome them (embodied in the increased popularity in approaches such as process philosophy).

Depicting truth as perspective offers opportunities to think about what it means to be human or socially independent from the dominance of science (which may explain its popularity amongst contemporary schools of critical thought). However, the view that truth is perspective also contrasts the extent to which knowledge can be understood as existing independently of the individual, which affects not only how we imagine the truths of the sciences but also excludes any collective truths that transcend the individual. Such positions are forced to exclude views that see language as inherited by the user (such as Chomsky) or as a consensual entity between users (such as Habermas). I do not wish to debate or unpick the intricacies of these entrenched positions as there are some important reasons as to why they have been prominent. However, as argued, at their most extreme all such interpretations pose a problem, for views that hold that there is no truth to language other than that which can be gained through interdependent consensus must contend with the increased possibility that any view on such perspectives may descend into relativism. For those who believe that language can hold truths beyond the individual, what is to resist any one truth becoming dogmatic? If language is what is used to assess the truth and seen as true at the same time, how can language be viewed independently to confirm or ascertain if it is in fact true or not (the problem is so potent that Popper and Wittgenstein are said to have almost come to blows with a red-hot poker after a similar discussion, Edmonds and Eidinow, 2001)? The more either side attempts to occupy a reasonable moderate position, the further they get from the medium, the middle ground here is always counter-intuitively contrasting. Therefore, to challenge thoughts access to the absolute opens up the heart of the debate to the concept of truth.

The method postulated approaches this problem in a novel way by using the contrast between concepts as a basis for analysing concepts independent of truth. As contrast is both in language whilst pre-emptive of language at the same time (i.e. it is sensed), it constitutes something beyond truth, a truth that is simultaneously not a truth. As can be seen from the table below:

**Figure II-5**

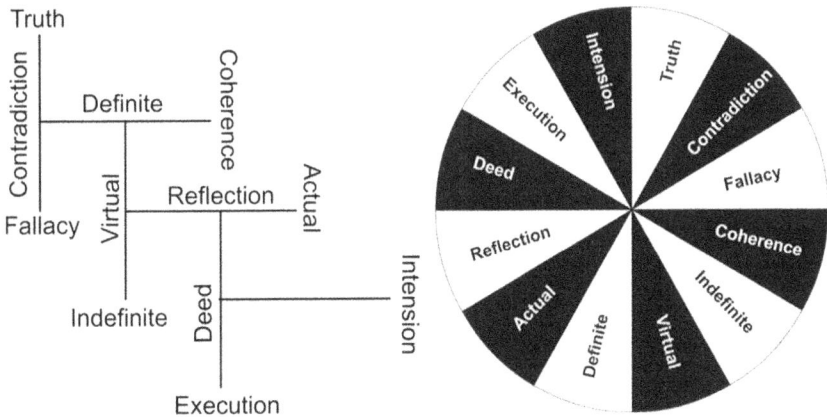

**Table II-4**

| Truth | Indefinite | Reflexive/thought |
|---|---|---|
| Truth is a hard concept to define because it must always be defined in reference to something else, like a fact, belief or value. Truth seeks to ascertain the consistency of something within the context of some other order of things. | Between contradiction and coherence is a state of the indefinite, something which is neither a contradiction nor yet coherent. | Between the virtual and the actual is reflexivity or thought. This concept is in between and is the place where the actual virtual meet. |
| | Definite | Execution |
| | The opposite of the indefinite is the state of something | The opposite of thought is to do, or to execute something. |

| Fallacy | being definite, something | This is a hard concept to put |
|---|---|---|
| Fallacy is the opposite of truth which highlights an inconsistency with a fact, belief or value in the context of some other order. | that is fully known.<br><br>Virtual<br><br>Between the indefinite and definite is the virtual. Something that may exist in a certain sense but refers to an existence that is not yet actual (could also be termed potentiality as used in Aristotle). | into words because it is whatever we do without thought it reflection which is by definition just doing.<br><br>Intension |
| Contradiction<br><br>The middle point between truth and fallacy is the concept of contradiction, beyond the dichotomy of truth and false where meaning loses sense. | | Between a thought and doing therefore is an intension, a preordained meaning.<br><br>Unintended |
| Coherence/Consistency<br><br>The opposite of contradiction is coherence. The point at which meaning becomes sensible. | Actual<br><br>The opposite of the virtual therefore is actual. Something that can be traced in the 'here and now'. | The opposite of an intension is something unintended, something that has not been preordained. Which brings us back to truth, as truth is the contrast between intension and that which happens to occur. Therefore, truths are found ascertaining the consistency between intensions and occurrences. |

The perspective gained on truth in the table is as absolute as it is relative, as each concept leads to another that then returns to the same one. This can be made clearer by distinguishing contradiction from contrast. At first contrast and contradiction may be seen as similar. However, the key difference demonstrated here is that contradiction should only be used in reference to language or logic leaving contrast to take on a broader meaning to denote the boundaries of sense beyond any one meaning. As a result, contradictions can be seen as eclipsing values in meaning, whereas contrast is always an affirmation of value, both in meaning and outside. If this distinction is made, it allows for their similarity whilst allowing each of them a distinct function. This allows for contrasts and contradictions to overlap, whereby a contradiction still has some jurisdiction over truth, whilst at the same time being subservient to a higher form of contrast of which it is informed by but can never be fully coherent with.

The complementary relationships between truth/nondeterminate and fallacy/reflection (on opposite sides of the wheel) seem to highlight a prime quality of truth. That truth is undetermined, and that it is within the context of thought or reflection that truth becomes fallacy. Non-determinacy is a difficult concept to conceptualise as it refers to an absolute state with ambiguous contrast. However, to conceptualise determinacy requires an ascertainment of where such a state begins and ends, as without this contrast the meaning of the concept becomes impossible (Brassier, 2013). Non-determinacy can be no more or less absolute than any other concept and must have its own contradiction; in this case, the concept of determinacy. Therefore, to believe in truth as undetermined requires a concept of determinacy that is related to non-determinacy, with both having the ability to succeed or supersede the other (in this way truth is a means to use meaning pragmatically, as can be read in American pragmatism's key theme of consequentialism). As a result, contrast must be both undetermined and determined at the same time. This challenges the naturalistic fallacy (of Moore, 1971): and exerts that truth exists as default (i.e. it is given), and fallacy as the exception. This could be imagined as an innocent child who knows nothing of innocence until encountering its contrast. This process of deriving fallacy from truth is implicit to the justification of scientific method as demonstrated by the 'principle of falsification'. If the classical goal of science is to prove specific hypothesis true, how can different hypothesises be judged as to whether they are true or not? Induction can be used to propose that hypothetical statements can be refined and narrowed down until they reach a universal truth that can be observed through scientific method. However, through this principle, as Hume and Kant pointed out, any hypothesis can never be fully verified as there may always be an outlying case that may have evaded the principle (this is known as the 'problem of induction'). Popper (1974) addressed this problem with the idea of falsification; that any hypothesis, statement or theory (including scientific) must be considered as falsifiable. Popper used this to argue that any statement that is non-falsifiable is incompatible with the scientific method, as it violates the cornerstones of scientific logic, rooted in observation rather than declaration. For Popper, falsification was used as a means by which to demarcate if a fact was scientific or not. This was refuted by Kuhn (1970) and Feyerabend (1993) who argued that falsification doesn't account for how science is also defined by the consensus of a scientific community. What this demonstrates is that the absence of fallacy doesn't result in truth, rather the two are in intimate relation with each other. Therefore, the obvious next step is to argue that statements that may at one time be considered false may also have the potential to be proven true.[6] If inverted the importance of exception is implied; the idea that we should always be willing to revise our beliefs in the light of new evidence (the importance of which is to avoid the myth of the categorial given, i.e. that truths are always already given to us see Christias, 2016).

Knowledge in this sense cannot exclude fideism and can never be certain of any one absolute truth without contrast as it is the relation between thought and that which is construed as in opposition to it through which things are made meaningful (Roubiczek, 1952). Truth is the process of assessing somethings part in something else. Therefore, knowledge is partial to the thinker but absolute as part of the universe taken as entire (universal), therefore both absolute and not at the same time. The result is a principle that both confirms as much as it denies sufficient reason (first formulated by Leibniz, 1890a), as to wholly verify sufficient reason one would have to view it from an impossible position of the entirety of the whole universe. As any one reason is only one part of the universe, that reason must be considered to be both consistent with the entire universe and entirely inconsistent with all other parts of it. Therefore, specific reason holds when taken as a whole, but the more any one individual reason is pressed, the more it results in contradiction as meaning is recursive (which highlights Hume's inductive problem with sufficient reason). Sufficient reason therefore presents existence as something that can be either proven reasonable or unreasonable denying indeterminate ways to view the world beyond this polemic. If sufficient reason (as with any reason) is only visible through contrast, it cannot be proven as reason will always spawn more reasons. Without contrast, there can be no meaning or reason at all and therefore no sufficient reason. Ironically if thought and meaning wasn't geared in this self-referential way, it wouldn't be able to derive sense from existence. But if there were no reason, i.e. there was no reason at all to anything, it would also be impossible to derive sense in any way at all or operate as a subject. And therefore, sufficient reason echoes contrast and is indeterminately both truth and fallacy.

This means that truth both is and isn't only ever one particular perspective (as presented in Nietzsche, 2003). In order for there to be a reflection, something entire and actual must exist (as is the basic premise behind questioning facticity). However, any one particular reflection is only ever a perspective; one particular aspect of the thing that it is reflecting. In this way, truth can be seen as something that only ever belongs to the individual. This is also a contradiction in terms however, as truth is also always unavoidable. Even when telling a lie one can never be detached from a truth. In thought existence is unmistakable and undeniable, the thinker may never know the exactness of what they are reflecting on but must at all times reflect something. Therefore, individual thought always gets to see truth through its relation to fallacy (a form of scepticism). Fallacy comes from the contrast of being an individual positioned in an existence that is both infinitely bigger and smaller than it (that also has a objectivity both a before and after it). This can be said to be both a perspective but can also never be individual perspective alone as Individual truths are contrasted against external fallacies (or vice versa), and the individual needs to contrast that which it reflects upon to make meaning. The concept of truth therefore must allow for its contradiction as truth derives from contrast. No one concept can ever be said to offer a wholly true, or a wholly false reflection, a concept is only ever a mediation between wider concepts and that from which all concepts are derived; contrast. Even if a reason can be said to have no literal truth, a reason may never be fully stripped of its symbolic value. Therefore, even if there is no one truth, we still know that truth exists as the fact that there is not only one truth alone is a truth.

There is no option to abandon or modify the concept of truth, rather it should be accepted as intimately related to contradiction. In order to understand the relationship between truth and reason as absolute, unrelated concepts cannot be used on their own. No true thought can be presented to our senses free from contrast (like Rumi's 2008 concept of the heart: "a donkey stuck in mud is logic's fate - Love's nature only love can demonstrate"). The contrast presented cannot be represented as one singular thing. The truths of these contrasts are buried between the cyclical relationships of concepts and their opposites never able to be fully explicated or disavowed. A concept (like the contrast it is derived from) is never merely true or false. Contrast is at the very point of change, and so true and false at the same time. Contrast denotes the point at which things become sense-able, yet it remains unclear as to whether contrast exists independently to the things that are themselves being used to imply the contrast. Is each contrast (sensed or un-sensed) different or are all contrasts exactly the same? And does contrast even exist at all as distinct? In this way concepts are an attempt to reflect form from contrast, which results in infinite possible positions to truth and fallacy like a mirror reflected upon itself or a *mis en abyme* (but eventually joining back together), implying there is no limit of nuance to truths. This can be compared to a perfect circle, or a perfectly straight line, or absolutely white light, or perfect randomness, no actuality can ever be claimed as their perfect example would denote infinite points, their only recourse to existence is from their idealisation (see Ingold, 2016 on lines). In this regard infinity is both ideal and actual as thought can deduct infinity for example from the colour spectrum or pi, yet by definition, it is impossible to actually quantify or prove. The only way to make actual meaning of the infinity implied by contrast is to break these reflections down in a cyclical series of evenly related concepts, in this case, 12 (as demonstrated through the method postulated). This understanding of truth therefore has an implication for the concept of value. If truth is contrast and contrast is infinite how can they have a value? As value relies upon a demarcated limit.

## Value

The argument so far has posed a dilemma. It has maintained that reflexive thoughts cannot assert the purity of concepts from contrast, meaning they are always somewhere between the rational and irrational; absolute and relative;

truth and fallacy at the same time. Adopting a position that understands the meaning of concepts through contrast, therefore, attempts to ensure that every meaning has a value. However, to believe in every value also surely means its opposite; to believe in nothing, as nothing must have a value. But how can nothing be nothing if it has a value? As a consequence, how is meaning or value created from such a relative position. From relativity, belief is impossible as how can one particular belief stand out from another? I have argued that rationality carries with it the ability to discern between different possible beliefs but carries no option of non-belief as to not believe constitutes another belief. Therefore, what use is the ability to be rational without direction? This problem is demonstrated by Hume (2004) in his distinction of 'ought from is', or put another way 'facts from values'. Originally posed by Hume to explain the limitations of humans to act free from 'unsubstantiated' belief. The distinction states that any 'ought' statements, even those derived from a fact, must invariably contain moral values. For almost three centuries the distinction has formed the corner stone of moral philosophy (and axiology) and proved critical in the social sciences by emphasising the inevitability of quality in rational arguments. The rhetoric dialectic method can be used to further elaborate the dichotomy. Once placed into a spectrum, the concept of facts and values must relate not just dualistically, from each other but also from a wider range of concepts. Such an attempt has been compiled below:

**Figure II-6**

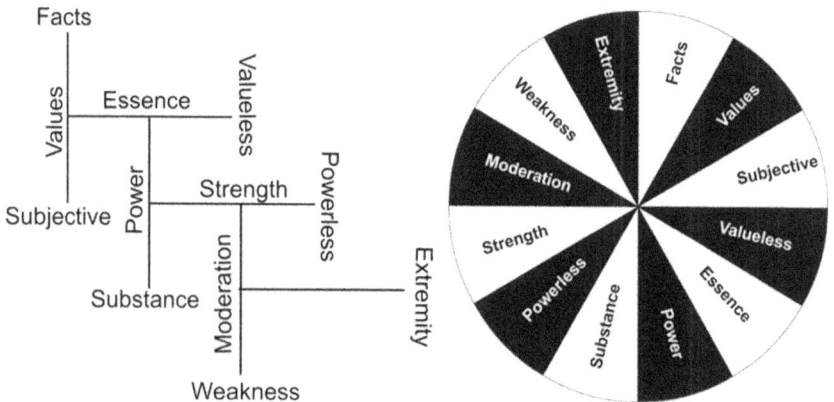

**Table II-5**

| Facts | Essence | Strength |
|---|---|---|
| The word 'fact' has several different meanings, but in the context of the discussion above the meaning is in sense of being objective.

**Subjective**

Opposed to objectivity is subjectivity.

**Values**

Therefore, value is not opposed to fact, it is to be found at the exact point between objectivity and subjectivity, and therefore value is equally subjective and objective whilst equally neither at the same time.

**Valueless**

The opposite of value is without value. This concept may have many negative connotations attached to it which we should be careful of when interpreting this spectrum not to distort the meaning of. | Between value and no value is essence. As essence is always illusive it can be described as the value of something, but at the same time, it is invaluable as it is unattainable (reminiscent of Walter Benjamin's notion of reproduction).

**Substance**

The opposite of essence is substance, the meaning of this concept may seem to be 'matter of fact' and given, however, as distinguished from the first concept of objectivity, this concept of substance is separate to value, and as such is just as much an extreme and unattainable concept. Therefore, substance is always given to us but not fully received unless consumed.

**Power**

That which is consumable from an object or subject, is therefore its power. Power therefore, is both the essential and the substantial, but also neither (could also be termed influence).

**Powerlessness**

The opposite of power is something lacking in power. | Between power and powerlessness must come strength, as if something is powerless yet resistant it must have some hidden strength which is beyond the power which is being exerted upon it.

**Weakness**

The opposite of strength is weakness. Powerlessness and weakness may often be associated together, but there is nothing inherent in weakness to say it lacks power, and indeed the powerful may also be weak.

**Moderation**

Between strength and weakness is moderation. When seeking to balance strengths and weaknesses, the outcome of this process is a moderation.

**Extremity**

The opposite of moderation is the extreme. Which is where one aspect of an object or subject is emphasised to the detriment of its other attributes. This brings us back to facts, as facts can be considered to be an extreme moderation or a moderate extreme. |

All of the concepts on the spectrum cannot be seen as either true or false, rather they all represent some sort of judgement of value. Therefore, all of the component concepts of the spectrum represent an extreme and unattainable position (which must also be true of all other spectrums). Belief is inevitable as individuals have no choice but to believe and not believing therefore constitutes a new belief. Therefore, belief must always be in the face of contradiction. This could again be assessed as a naturalistic fallacy; that once human belief is stripped from the world, what is left behind must be true (Moore, 1971). However, when considering that this level of purity is not possible, it must be assumed that truth doesn't exist in isolation. If it is accepted that truth and fallacy are non-exclusive, it becomes possible to distinguish facts from values, as the world according to, and the world independent from the individual are undetermined without contrast. The spectrum above nuances the position that can be taken towards the concepts, as it provides a list of concepts with which to further qualify facts from values. Any fact/value judgements cannot avoid assuming a position between facts and values on the spectrum; that position can never be one concept alone free of contrast, and therefore fact/value judgements are conducted between these positions and never simply true or false without exception. This can be received as instigating a need to either come to terms with subjectivity, or find a way to reassert objectivity. This is tricky without implying a dualism however, as objectivity is accessed by subjectivity and vice versa. One means to address this would be to evoke a pragmatic point, facts and value are not separated or divided into two camps they are the result of a process formed through the position of a specific subjectivity (see James, 2015). Subjectivity implies a relation to reality in which the subject is surrounded by things both bigger and smaller than it (spatially as well as temporally). The unassailability of the subject/object distinction is reflected in the fact that all attempts to rectify facts from values become self-fulfilling (and so also cyclical).

This differs significantly to contemporary continental trends in speculative realism that wish to assert an absolute free from subjective values by reopening Locke's (1998) related delineation of primary and secondary properties. Primary properties are properties of objects independent of any observation, whereas secondary properties are properties that produce sensation in observers (i.e. are objective or subjective). Criticisms that have obscured the primary/secondary distinction are similar to ones already presented and have stemmed from the argument that an observer can never become independent to their observation as to do so would be another observation. In recognising these criticisms, speculative realism has sought to create new positions for philosophy that are conscious of the obfuscatory nature of the subject/object distinction but make possible a revival of the debate around primary and secondary properties. E.g. for Meillassoux (2009) this has meant arguing towards ways in which maths can demonstrate things in themselves (beyond knowledge derived from the senses in the style of empiricism), or for object-oriented ontology (Bryant et al., 2010) it is to reject privileging human existence over the existence of nonhuman objects. Such positions wish to question the points raised by the 'correlationalist' philosophies (more precisely; idealism; phenomenology; post-structuralism) that have made realism difficult. But to do so have needed to experiment with classical laws of thought and debate the necessity of the laws of nature to be contingent. Such depictions render reality as a sort of hyper-chaos without the subject at its centre.

The method postulated draws clear parallels to these trends wishing to access existence anterior to the subject, but is made distinct by subjugating both contradiction and reason (and all other concepts) as existing a posteriori to the contrast which forms their demarcation. I argue that when searching for objects independent to the observer what is highlighted is more and more contrast. If any given contrast between things has an indeterminate beginning and end then it implies that contrast is infinite, which means that it contains an infinity of forms when scaled up or down. Proposing contingency alone as implying infinity (as Meillassoux does) raises questions about whether its physical existence can be considered as actual (see Hallward, 2011), the infinity of contrast however, exists as physical and tangent. Such an infinity offers more than enough resource to comprise all thoughts and concepts, as well as demarcate all things from each other. To contrast, the position of the subject and object cannot be discarded as it demarcates the boundaries of contrast. However, using contrast, both thought and existence become distinguishable apart from the other.

The independence of contrast is the very thing from which thought standardises and regulates itself on. If thought and being are made distinct through contrast, it is possible to imagine ourselves as totally distinct from the universe we inhabit whilst integrally part of it at the same time. Rather than concepts ever proving things in themselves, it is highlighting relationships derived from contrast. So, in one way things in themselves can never be known in as much as there are things in themselves to know, in another way it is impossible to avoid knowing things in themselves as the contrast sensed in thought is (and isn't) such a thing in itself. Contrast in this sense is present in every sense and sensation from the loftiest thought to the basest of subconscious impulses. This link is even present in the most elementary of observations of contrast possible between particles, and so the question becomes where the physical begins and ends and how does the physical world relate to all the principles reflected in observable things throughout being (a point that will be picked up upon later in the section on existence). If we imagine our thoughts are integrally linked to the relationship between the contrast observable in all objects, they must also become reflections of that relationship and so the same as the physical world whilst not the same as that from which they are derived.

This understanding means that contrast must be seen as both relational and preeminent of any relation. This point is similar to Harman (2016, chap. 5) when arguing that the question of primary properties independent from a human observer, is to find an object free of any relations altogether. This changes the search for the properties of objects as independent to find objects that maintain the same identity regardless of its relation. To this point, the same conclusion could be offered, that the only thing not to have a relation is buried deep within contrast. Contrast is not nothingness and not the totality of something but a result of the two. To consider the relationality of contrast is a contradiction in terms therefore, because it is pure relation, the result of two things interacting with each other, yet distinct, infinite and unchanging on the other. If it is possible to distinguish a contrast at what point does the contrast differ from the things causing that contrast? In this way, contrast becomes like nothing else, both possible to sense and able to cause effect whilst ephemeral and derived from the properties of other things. To imagine existence presupposing of unity (as Hegel), or as imminence (as Deleuze) with no contrast to anything is to imagine existence as totally static resulting in a world of no things at all as there is nothing to distinguish things from each other (in other words a non-thinkable existence). Therefore, contrast is a prerequisite of both thought and thought of existence. It is in the contrast that we are to find the only true total independence from thought, and contrast can neither be said as relational or not. As a result, objects can only be considered to exist only in as much as they are able to evoke a contrast, regardless of the observer.

This opens the question of how empirical methods and science connects to idealism. Does science need to be tied to truths as non-contrasting? Or in finding absolute truths? And was the search for things 'in themselves' ever particularly scientific in the first place? The demise of the philosophy of nature conceived by Schelling and Hegel demonstrated that concepts such as unity or contradiction were incompatible with empiricism conceived as unbiased. This is why contrast is inherently more useful here, as it places very little emphasis on observations to exist in a certain way, only that observations demonstrate a minimum of difference from their surroundings. Therefore, a focus on the meaning of contrast itself is an attempt to get right to the source and undercut biases arising from logic, emotion, reason or circumstance. Contrast asserts that all there is, is until it isn't, providing an onus that all meaningful existence must pass through. This need not imply unity, consistency or eternal return (e.g. Simmel and Kaufmann demonstrated that three circles rotating could be configured in finite space and infinite time to never return to a straight line). But it does imply a certain amor fati that things are the way they are until proven through contrast.

Freed from the constraint of logocentrism the facts/value distinction is no longer confined to describing moral contradictions, as if to say the distinction is only ever relevant to a human subject (as in the positions of existentialism) but the distinction must also stem from each anterior contrast. What is highlighted is something about the nature from which meaning derives. The question becomes one of tracing the properties of contrast, and identifying how contrast is used to distinguish one thing from another. In this trail of thought, the correlation between the world anterior and interior to the human collapses as all things share the same relation to contrast. If there is no contrast then there can be no object or event (or experience) as contrast makes both cognisable (a point that can be linked to Bergson's 1999 contrast of time with space, or Whitehead's 2015 bifurcation 'breach' of the order of subject – object). Without contrast, thought is unimaginable as it has no means with which to perpetuate or regulate itself. Therefore, the contrast found in meaning must reflect the contrasts of matter exterior to it. This is to say that reality is more than just our interpretation of it, but also that all interpretation is as much a reality as anything else. Therefore, the important question should not be if analysis is 'realist', 'correlationalist' or 'Idealist' (quantitative or qualitative, reductionist or pluralist, positive or interpretivist), as however this distinction is interpreted, it is unavoidable to concede that it implies that contrast is inherent to both human thought and whatever is contrasting it. Rather, we should consider the conditions necessary whereby all of these positions can be meaningfully posed. Ultimately, without an appreciation of contrast thought has no position of the contrast to link all propositions together.

This results in an intriguing perspective on contrast, but one that is already so familiar to all of us it is second nature. The question, therefore, is not how to get beyond this contrast, but rather also how to accept it as peremptory. The method so far compiled demonstrates some insight on the cyclical nature of meaning, but how can this insight (that is as limiting as it is insightful and as mundane as it is revelatory) be taken further?

**Table II-6**

| |
|---|
| **Chapter Summary:**<br>To clarify the argument before moving on, below are some key points highlighted by the method in this chapter:<br><br>• Emotion, Logic and Reason are a sense of contrast.<br>• Concepts cannot be used to represent a total absolute beyond their own meaning, as |

when looking for absolutes the more we find contrasts that leave something aside from representation.

- The line between truths and fallacies, and facts and values is transitory and may never be considered to be neutral. All meaning is meaningful until rendered otherwise by contrast.
- Contradiction is a cancellation of all value, whereas contrast is an affirmation of value.

Contrast cannot be considered to be either objective or subjective, and contrast is independent yet dependent to both an object or subject.

## Endnotes

[1] The science of pain (sense) already questions the Cartesian model of a sense being sensed in the body and making its way to the brain, as the brain can also be seen to have role in preparing the state of the body to receive pain. See the 'Mature organisms Model'.

[2] Therefore, thought is not one and contained as in Aristotle, or defined wholly by its relation to itself, but somewhere in the exact middle of these two processes.

[3] "That true and positive meaning of the antinomies is this: that every actual thing involves a coexistence of opposed elements. Consequently to know, or, in other words, to comprehend an object is equivalent to being conscious of it as a concrete unity of opposed determinations. The old metaphysic, as we have already seen, when it studied the objects of which it sought a metaphysical knowledge, went to work by applying categories abstractly and to the exclusion of their opposites." (Hegel, 2015, sec. IV)

[4] Some readings of Hegel are more radical than others which may alter the ways in which this point is considered. One interpretation is to consider Hegel's philosophy as totalising (the so-called French interpretation), or to read Hegel as supremely contingent. Some very compelling readings of Hegel already develop the tension in Hegel's work between the 'end of history' and the 'cunning of reason' to suggest the necessity of contingency. For example see Burnbidge (2007) or Hahn (2007) or Padui (2010) or Mabil (2013). Rather than an understanding of dialectic as offering greater consciousness, my aim is to develop the latter understanding of dialectic as always elusive. However, rather that attempt to tie dialectic to one mode or concept alone the perspective I am attempting is of an exclusion that even confounds reason itself and concepts such as contingency.

[5] Or Johnson's criticism of Berkeley: "After we came out of the church, we stood talking for some time together of Bishop Berkeley's ingenious sophistry to prove the non-existence of matter, and that every thing in the universe is merely ideal. I observed, that though we are satisfied his doctrine is not true, it is impossible to refute it. I never shall forget the alacrity with which Johnson answered, striking his foot with mighty force against a large stone, till he rebounded from it, 'I refute it thus.'"

[6] This is not the view taken by Popper who sought to create an account free of idealism and also block dialectic as somehow superior to logic (Popper, 1940). What is more, Popper can be placed in a larger movement of analytic philosophers seeking to founder logic allied to scientific knowledge as distinct and supreme from other forms of knowledge. It is for this reason that my adotption of Popper here (and the subsequent debates and studies he prompted) is to adopt the stance that falsification prompts: a scepticism implying that no one knowledge alone is supreme, but to reject that this stance is characterised in formal logic or science alone.

Chapter III

# Essence

*"To see the world in a grain of sand and heaven in a wild flower, hold
infinity in your hand and eternity in an hour"* (William Blake)

The previous section discussed how the method postulated can be used to
elucidate sense and meaning from contrast, this section will discuss meanings
ambiguous relationship to matter (vis-à-vis the physical). To do this, it
explores a range of concepts such as narrative, pattern and contrast that
bridge the line between the meaning and matter. Rather than place meaning
or matter in any one of these concepts however, it looks at what can be
deduced from the contrast between them. This feat is difficult to reason as it
must make tangible that which is used to make meanings relatable. This
chapter will further explore meaning outside of individual thought and
language by looking at the concept of meaning, and then a series of concepts
that imply meanings beyond verbal expression. More precisely; narrative;
pattern; the concept of existence itself; and contrast.

## Meaning

Meaning has so far been presented as not being fully contained in language.
In dialectic, meaning is presented as defined by the opposition, whilst
rhetoric is presented as asserting that meaning cannot be exhausted in finite
expression. An explanation of semantics or semiotics as the activity of placing
different signs (or referents) on to signifiers and committing them to memory
does not address how the memories of each sign distinguish themselves from
each other.[1] An appreciation of contrast is required to make meanings stand
out from one another and in some way prefigure the meaning. Current
semiotics or semantics is required to take a position between a belief that
words are arbitrary and independent of what they signify; or that there must
be some type of external connection between a signifier and what it signifies
(in positions such as naturalism). This enquiry in some way has accompanied
Plato's ideal forms, and the scholastics, and has more recently been the
subject of both continental philosophy in the form of structuralism and
analytical philosophy such as the Frege-Russell v Kripke-Putnam theories of
reference. Emphasising contrast's importance to meaning reveals that none of
these propositions can be seen to be merely true or false. If contrast is
something independent to the subject but also sensed, contrast can be used

as the basis for all meaning. The question then becomes focused on the contrast. Is contrast something which can be found throughout all matter connecting matter to meaning, or is contrast innate, only felt by lifeforms and bears no resemblance to the world around it? Contrast must oppose matter or else there could be no existence from which to think in (there would be only constancy). At the same time, contrast must oppose thought or there would be no existence outside of thought, giving contrast an ambiguous presence.

In the 20th century, methodologies of the social sciences and humanities portrayed meaning as exclusive to language (named the linguistic turn by Rorty, 2002). In the hindsight of the early 21st century, the difficulty of reconciling an individual's own personal interpretation with any other over-arching reality has been identified as a limitation of these movements. As a result, continental philosophy has fragmented further into positions which continue the search for nuance in language and communication (such as those in the philosophy of communication Arneson, 2007) and new 'materialisms' seeking to look exclusively at material as a means to forge new lines of philosophical enquiry (such as in pragmatism Egginton and Sandbothe, 2004; or the so-called speculative turn Bryant et al., 2010). The search for meaning in material is ultimately the search for meaning outside of language. In such a search, the means by which things become definable and distinguishable is of chief concern, as without definition there is no point or justification to thought. However, in breaching the issue, we can question whether contemporary philosophy is contradicting the linguistic turn only to assume one side of another dualism between material and language. To investigate this question the contradiction should be assumed and embraced more fully. For example, instead of reasoning that if being is not matter, then it must be all meaning, or that if being is not meaning it must be matter, what comes of suggesting a further position: being is as much as it isn't matter and meaning? A clue lies in the double entendre of the word 'matter' – as material and significance (and also reflected in its etymology from mater, mother or origin). For example, why should meaning be seen to 'matter' any more or less than anything else? Neither meaning nor material (whether observed or not) can be determined aside from the contrast that denotes that things matter. Both meaning and matter are made distinguishable through contrast, without contrast there is no means for them to stand out. No singular point can be traced where matter separates from meaning, as they both evolved from the recursion of contrast over aeons until forming impulses, and feelings that eventuate into more and more complex languages. Therefore, meaning is both matter and not matter at the same time, as it derives from the contrast of matter contra matter. Meaning is what matters from matter. To investigate further, the method postulated has been applied to the concept of meaning below:

**Figure III-1**

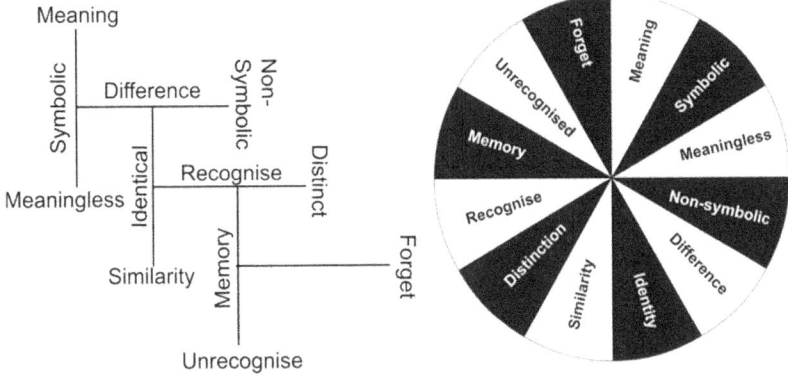

**Table III-1**

| Meaning | Difference | Recognise |
|---|---|---|
| To express something as meaningful.<br><br>Meaningless (or matter)<br><br>The opposite of meaning is to express something that does not mean anything.<br><br>Symbolic<br><br>Between meaning and meaninglessness is the symbolic, something with transportable meaning. Therefore, an object that is both meaningful and meaningless.<br><br>Non-symbolic<br><br>The opposite of the symbolic is the non-symbolic, something as it is with no symbolic value. This concept is significant if wishing to allude to the world without the observer. | Between the symbolic and non-symbolic is difference, which is the amount to which things are dissimilar to each other. I.e. symbolic or not of one another.<br><br>Similarity<br><br>The opposite of difference is similarity, which is the amount to which things resemble each other.<br><br>Identical<br><br>Between similarity and difference is something that is indistinguishable from something else. In English, this word also holds the connotation of the Greek word idios i.e. to own; meaning that the identity of something must be claimed by something related to it.<br><br>Distinct<br><br>The opposite of something identical is something distinct, something distinguishable from something else. | In between the identical and the distinct is recognition, the ability to distinguish between things that would otherwise be entirely identical.<br><br>Unrecognisable<br><br>The opposite of recognition is to not recognise, to not distinguish something from its surroundings.<br><br>Memory<br><br>Between recognition and non-recognition is memory, as memory is the ability to recall previous cognitions of the past to allow for a comparison in current cognition for comparison with the subject of cognition.<br><br>Forget<br><br>The opposite of memory is to forget; to lose memories. This function is important in the process of creating new memories. Meaning is the force behind this ordering between memory and forgettability. |

To interpret the results, meaning should again be related to contradiction and negation. For much of the history of Western philosophy, contradiction has been seen as a threat to meaning. The law of non-contradiction originating in classical thought (Aristotle, 1998), enforces a strict rule on logic that contradictory statements cannot be held as true in the same sense at the same time. Logical interpretations of this law deem it as implying that contradiction equates to meaninglessness. Contradiction according to logical interpretations does not adjudicate the meaning or value of truth and fallacy, rather its meaning is reduced to the meaning of fallacy alone. In this light Western philosophy engaging contradiction can be seen to reiterate over and again a playoff of contradictions because it has proceeded as if 'existence' was something to resolve with logic or reason (or render compatibly into one system of thought). Many accounts have even taken this concern as central to their position (for example in post modernism's experimentations with perspectivism and quarrels with grand narratives or Actor Network Theory's advocation of multiple ontologies). Only being aware of this tendency however, is not enough to think beyond it, as any attempt at resolution is another attempt to render a contradiction as comparable to truth. The attempt to resolve contradiction obscures wider meanings of a contradiction as an undefined intermediary. Meaning relies upon having a value above that of which it is referring to. The maintenance of this higher value requires contradiction as a means to disqualify meanings whilst still allowing them some meaning. As such accounts must avoid implying a trivial position whereby all contradictions are true resulting in meaning descending into absurdity (notable examples are Azzouni, 2003; Kabay, 2008). Or at the opposite extreme to advocate extreme cynicism whereby all meanings are to be assumed false. Avoiding these dangers requires thought to take seriously experience outside of logic and demote logic alone as supreme. This necessitates a sort of Pyrrhonian scepticism (of Aenesidemus and Agrippa via Sextus Empiricus, 2000), that no one thing should be considered inherently either true or false on its own, it is through reflection that things gain meaning.

Scientific method and mathematics have had a different relationship to contradiction as they do not problematise the link between meaning and matter as directly. Many contradictions can be observed meaningfully through experiment, which are often at odds with classical logic (like the decimal places of pi, fractals, or quantum mechanics). However, even scientific method and mathematics are at odds when faced with meanings biggest contradiction; the total un-observability of nothingness. The concept of nothing is supremely enigmatic, as nothingness enforces a limit on observation (i.e. how can nothing be observed as any observation of it implies a something), but at the same time, nothing is meaningful without the concept of nothing (Priest, 2006a). The interpretations of experiments and observations are as much enslaved by the limits of meaning as everything else thought or sensed. The question, 'why is there something rather than nothing' (first raised by Leibniz, 1890b) can be broached in a number of ways through experiment. What was once thought to be nothing has been transformed over and again by discoveries such as oxygen, gravity, space/time, or more recently hyperspace, dark matter and how elementary particles may rise in and out of existence (see Greene, 2000; and Krauss, 2014).[2] However, once any concept of nothing is debunked as actually containing something it must be replaced by a new concept of nothingness as a semantic necessity to make sense of the newly discovered part of existence (such is Quine's 1948 criterion of ontological commitments). For nothingness to be knowable would require the concept to be absolute and total (as nothingness would be infinite), but such a position could no longer ascribe (or make distinct or definable) value, as values rely upon the unknown and the finite.

Meaning, therefore, is not nothing (i.e. nihilistic), it is in some way part of the things that exist, the so-called physical world yet it is also in contrast to it. Language that is stable and free of contrast or contradiction is a paradox.[3] Meaning seen in this light can never be neutral, as the thought required to ponder it relies on the contradiction it is attempting to resolve and proves that the simple act of thinking at all is precisely what will always stop anything that can be experienced from reaching a totally stable, uncontradictable definition (see Chomsky, 2010 and the role of recursion in linguistics).[4] In this way, contrast can again be distinguished from contradiction; whereas contrast is sensed (not part of the body, not fully the outside world), contradiction is only ever reasoned, it is the reflection of the sense of infinite contrast and therefore inversed, made finite and totalised. A non-contradiction reasoned is an attempt to reflect on an indeterminate contrast. An expression of contradiction is an attempt to reflect contrast as totalised (i.e. eclipsing opposing meanings), as we know contrast is infinitely elusive and therefore escapes any attempts of totalisation. This can be easily demonstrated with language as meanings require contrasts that are not only contradictions. This then is the danger of contradiction; it is posed as absolute but by definition, it must always be partial (and as such, Kant and Hegel's opposing stances on contradiction – or antimony – cease to be exclusive, contradiction can be considered to highlight both a limit as well as the limit providing the conditions and content of reason). Non-contradiction therefore, is a means by which to think in a reality only perceivable through contrast. This process can be more familiarly understood to us as narrative. Narrative is the means to make sense of contrast, to render contrast as non-contradictory and whole.

## Narrative

Narrative is a key aspect of making sense and meaning. Narrative circumvents the totality of contradiction by extracting it out into a structure that is

recursive (and infinite). Through narrative concepts are linked together into
an arc or structure that has a meaning in addition to the meanings of the
constitutive concepts. The concept of a narrative therefore is at once personal
as well as extending the individual into something bigger. However, since the
scientific revolution narrative has been removed exclusively to the realm of
human thought. A good example of this is in Weber's (1997) vision of
enlightenment; if 'facts' are perceived as existing in a 'disenchanted' world
independent of human thought, narrative can only exist in the imagination of
humans (Josephson-Storm, 2017 offers a good overview of the subject).[5] As a
result, narrative has a conflicted status in the human sciences. Where some
approaches interpret the role of the human sciences as a means to separate
'reality' from narrative, the terminology of narrative is avoided (Lakoff and
Johnson, 1981). Other (existential- i.e. human subjective) postmodern or
phenomenological perspectives contribute to this by arguing that it is
impossible for a human subject to represent reality free of narrative (Barthes,
2009; Gadamer, 2004; Ricoeur, 1990b).

   In both such approaches, narrative is attributed to the mind, and in that sense
only exists to bring the wider world into meaning, therefore assuming that
narrative is only of the 'human' interpretive world'. As a result, the analysis of
narrative conducted in the spirit of Barthes (or Benjamin would be another
good example) tends to demonstrate the implicit fallacy behind every narrative,
whilst focusing less on any truths they may represent (O'Banion, 1991).
Criticisms have focused on how this has led to a crisis in academic belief in the
times since postmodernity, i.e. that all belief is relative and that no truth exists
beyond a particular narrative. As accounts have attempted to find what makes
narratives distinct, fewer contemporary accounts have presented what may be
similar to all narratives in the style of figures of the past such as Mircea Eliade or
Jean-Pierre Vernant. Joseph Campbell (1989) offers a counter example when
describing mythology as the "song of the universe, the music of the spheres".
According to this perspective, narrative plays a function in making things
meaningful by reflecting patterns found throughout existence, and so in this
sense, each narrative must also have some truth (or actuality) to them. If we
extend such a perspective, rather than arguing for narrative as universal or
culturally specific (or structural or post-structural) narrative conventions can be
linked to the dialectic recursion of contrasting concepts in the style seen in the
method presented. Over time meaning, language, myth and narrative may be
seen as emerging together in dialectical/rhetorical processes that are both
biological (i.e. part of a collective unconscious going back aeons) as well as
cultural (i.e. fully flexible, malleable in the here and now). A narrative's meaning
positions the human against what has emanated beyond them. The form of
narrative must contrast a pattern that runs through the whole of existence
against the situatedness of the individual. I do not wish to suggest that

everything is narrative, but that narrative aligns wider patterns outside of individual thought to individual thought:

**Figure III-2**

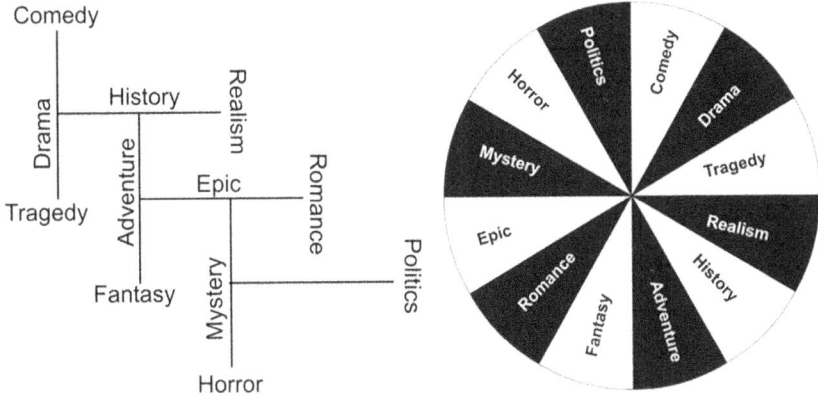

**Table III-2**

| Comedy | History/biography | Epic/Saga |
|---|---|---|
| The concept of comedy belies that reality is trivialised and the characters tend to be portrayed with sympathy. According to Aristotle comedy focuses on human weaknesses and foibles and of is less concerned with people's virtues. | Between drama and realism is a form of narrative that seeks to make sense of the story of a person. And as a person must make sense of themselves through drama, that which they create and reality that which created them, the result is a narrative. And that narrative most closely resembles the process of what we call history or biography. | The combination of adventure and romance is an epic or saga, of which some effort is made to capture the essential characteristics of the character(s). The overall characteristic of a saga therefore – in agreement with Aristotle – is that all events are serious and important and only overcome by the virtues or changing virtues of the lead character(s). |
| **Tragedy** | | **Horror** |
| The opposite concept of tragedy therefore portrays a narrative as overly serious and important and tends to portray characters as virtuous. | **Fantasy** | The opposite of a saga is horror, as horror is to imagine the narrative of existence without human characteristics. |
| **Drama** | The opposite of history/biography is fantasy which is narrative of the imagination. Which is real enough to be meaningful, but full of cathartic dramatic embellishment. | **Mystery/Thriller** |
| In between comedy and tragedy comes drama. Drama is point where comedy and tragedy become indistinguishable. | | In between a saga and horror is mystery or thriller. The focus of |

| Realism/documentary | Adventure/Action | this narrative is for the character(s) subject to find something out there beyond themselves and to understand or get to the bottom of the mystery. |
|---|---|---|
| The opposite of drama is therefore realism, this is a form of narrative that seeks to strip all forms of drama and embellishment from its representation. | In between history/biography and fantasy is adventure or action, which seeks to create a narrative that bends to the will of the character(s) or subject involved. | |
| | Romance | Politics |
| | The opposite of an action adventure therefore is to be involved in a narrative where a force bigger that the character(s) or subject are driving the narrative. | The opposite of a mystery therefore is a narrative that begins from the mundane existence of the character(s) or subject and to change it in some way advantageously for the subjects. Between a mystery and politics comes a comedy, where the mundane existence of the characters are trivialised against the mysteries of the universe. |

The narratives in this spectrum are most commonly associated with literary genres, however, here they suggest that narrative has a wider applicability. For example, the definitions of realism, politics and history are closely related in the spectrum. What must be avoided is to suggest that the drama of these narrative forms makes them any less real or objective, as drama must be as dependent on contrast as all the other concepts are. If drama is considered to not be real, and reality is considered to be devoid of drama, both subjective and objective expression lose their medium for meaning (which is a juxtaposition made more acute by scientific realism). Each narrative style is defined by the other. Therefore, the perspective of narrative gained by the table above is broader than that limited to literary genres and must include concepts such as ideology and argument as variants of the same thing (like Benjamin's 2015 concept of history).

The existence of narrative implies that there is something that totally encompasses ourselves, whilst also only ever being subject to us at the same time. Just as humans make sense of that which is external to them, so too must there be something external upon which it is possible to bring together in meaning. This highlights the idea of there being a world out there independent of us, yet inaccessible without some sort of narrative. Contemporary developments in speculative realism thematise the incommensurability of what may exist without narrative never to be sensed, linking this insight to speculative fiction (Thacker, 2011) and even to nihilism

(Brassier, 2007). However, here I do not wish to overplay the discoordination between the thought and reality, as just as thought must contrast the world it reflects in order to be able to think within it, thought must also be mutually and inescapably be attached to the world. Whether reality is considered as direct or indirect (i.e. the perception of distal physical objects or merely a phenomenological experience) human thought or narrative can never get too close to, or too far away from the world ulterior to it, thought is perpetually locked in a relationship that is co-narrated with the world it reflects. Just as a perfect circle can be imagined but never rendered physically without imperfection, so too does narrative allude to a form language is never able to capture fully (evoking Plato's ideal forms and sacred geometry). This interpretation provides more than a pragmatic interpretation of humans and objects as non-definitive beyond the processes by which they come to exist (typified by philosophies of process and becoming such as Deleuze, Whitehead and James).[6] It alludes to a form and meaning beyond language.

The method proposed allows for a more nuanced perspective of narrative as both within and beyond the subject. The perspective gained adheres to the same set of contrasting principles through which concepts perpetuate. Concepts and narratives are demonstrated to be intricately linked and rely on each other for meaning. A narrative is unattainable without a concept and concepts cannot be regulated and become corruptible without narrative. In this way, both narratives and concepts are concerned with defining problems and finding their solution. The role of narrative can be epitomised in the phrase, 'making ends meet'. Usually, this idiom of unknown origin has a negative connotation and is taken to mean enduring hardships to 'make a living'. When its wider etymology is considered however, it alludes to bringing things together and making them more stable, secure and practicable. This can be likened to the building, destruction and rebuilding of narratives. What would otherwise be seen as a series of random contradictions is made practicable through narrative (another idiom doing fulfilling a similar kind of function would be 'your days are numbered').

The concepts of realism, history or politics may seem to be less partial than other narratives, as the focus of these concepts could be said to be express attempts to view the world free from the belief and value of any one subject. Even for figures such as Walter Benjamin and the Analis School who argued that history or politics are never free from narrative, the idea of narrative they had in mind may differ from the restrictive set of prescribed narratives in the spectrum above. As a result, it allows us to combine positions that were hitherto contrary. If each narrative reflects reality, such a reflection only demonstrates one aspect of the reality which it represents. Therefore, narratives are never totally real or unreal as they are partial to their initial reflection. As reflections, narratives must be connected and inter-compatible, and when narratives meet, they must transform like colours blending. Far from each narrative being an isolated reflection, narrative must already be formed in ways in which it is intuitively transformative. For example, even the proclamation that there is no such thing as narrative does not escape becoming yet another narrative. A narrative's form is defined by the contrast which it is demarcated against, and each time a narrative is contrasted, a new narrative is created. This link with contrast means that understanding narrative is as much empirical as it is rational or ideological. Unlike logic, which defines itself against contradiction, narrative has a more encompassing and adaptative stance to contradictory propositions. In this way, history or politics (or any of the other narrative forms above) are incapable of being experienced without the contrasting interpretive forms of the other narratives. Observable events must be conducted in ways compatible with and fulfilling the necessity of narratives. The number of possible narratives therefore, is infinite and particular to their circumstance, however, when collected these infinite nuances separate out into distinct narrative forms. Like when zooming out of a pixelated photo, the form becomes apparent once viewed in aggregate to the point where individual nuances are indistinguishable. Therefore, narrative doesn't only exist in interpretation, but is structured in the world and nature around us through contrast.

In this schema, the results of the method postulated become paradoxical, we must accept a narrative which is partial in order to understand the ways in which narratives are impartial. When individually deployed both dialectic and rhetoric can endlessly reproduce different narratives. Conversely, the cyclical relationship between concepts is only distinguishable through the simultaneous deployment of both dialectic and rhetoric. This reveals the main difference between a concept and a narrative; each concept has an equal and opposite meaning, whereas a narrative doesn't necessarily have to be opposed (or at least it is not yet possible to understand this symmetry). Therefore, concepts are more elemental, and narrative is comprised by concept. Narrative is what connects the space between concepts, and in this sense, joins both the meaningful to the meaningless. If concepts use a pattern regulated throughout nature, a narrative relates those patterns together. This puts narrative in a peculiar position as it must navigate a space between where meaning and whatever opposes meaning meet. Therefore, the perspective of narrative whether 1st, 2nd or 3rd person is always between a subject and object. As a result, narrative can no better or worse describe an individual to themselves than describe what surrounds them in the outside world. This feature has led to the portrayal of narrative as unavoidable whilst also partial and only ever occupying one perspective (for example, 'the god eye view from nowhere' as described by Nagel, 1989).[7] However, if meaning can be demonstratable in a pattern, narrative must be related to the ways these patterns can be understood, giving a perspective on narrative that is empirical as well as ideal.

## Patterns and Problems

This section builds on the previous sections of meaning and narrative by looking at the concept of a pattern. Concepts and narratives are difficult to define when considering that all knowledge must be conducted in accordance with the workings of concept and narrative. The ability to compile concepts and narratives relies on the existence of some form of meaningful external pattern. Whilst the ability to identify and reflect upon this pattern relies upon the person reflecting to attain the concept of a pattern. This would imply that concepts are in a pattern of reflecting on a pattern. Similarly, if narrative joins concepts together in a pattern, this would imply that narrative has its own pattern of being the solution to a problem which leads to new problems. Therefore, the concept of patterns, problems and solutions must be intrinsically linked with and describe the transformation of meaning:

**Figure III-3**

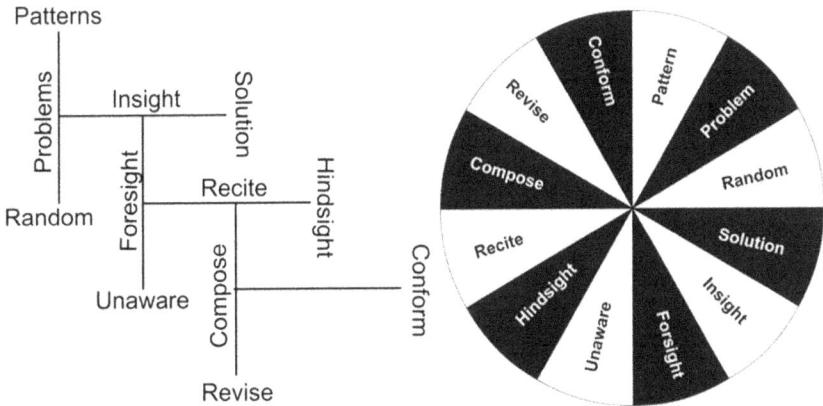

**Table III-3**

| Pattern | Insight | Recite |
| --- | --- | --- |
| A pattern is a regular and intelligible form or sequence discernible in the way which something happens or is done. | Between a problem and a solution is an insight. Which is the ability to understand a particular pattern and | Between hindsight and foresight is the ability to have knowledge previous and pre-emptive knowledge of a |

| Chaos | problem and even its solution. | pattern or problem etc. and therefore to be able to recite it at will. |
|---|---|---|
| The opposite of a pattern is entropic, which seemingly does not make sense and no known regularity can be found.[8] | Unaware | Revise |
| Problem | The opposite of an insight is to be in a pattern or problem etc. whilst not being aware of it. | The opposite of reciting is to revise, which is to alter the scrip of the pattern or problem etc. rather than merely recite it. |
| In between a pattern and chaos is a problem. In this sense, a problem is capable of being defined as a problem through its inability to fit into a pattern. | Hindsight | Compose |
| | Between insight and unawareness is hindsight, which is the experience of being aware of a pattern or problem etc. once you are not directly experiencing it. | Between recite and revise is to compose which is to both recite and revise patterns or problems into new patterns or problems etc. |
| Solution | Foresight | Conform |
| The opposite of a problem is a solution, which is the resolution of a problem. | The opposite of hindsight is foresight, which is the ability to pre-empt a pattern or problem etc. | To conform is to recite a pattern or problem etc. with no will but to conform. |

The above results demonstrate an insight to the point where meaning meets whatever is responsible for regulating it. For any attempt to define the underlying nature of reality, randomness is a major problem. When the theory of relativity was faced with the randomness implied by quantum entanglement Einstein is famously quoted as saying that he is quite certain that 'god does not play dice with the universe', and the incompatibility remained one of the major preoccupations of physics. If existence is ordered and principled (i.e. in a pattern), this would present a paradox to the meaning of the concepts of chaos, randomness or problems. Order in this sense would mean that randomness or problems conform to some sort of pattern that is yet to be discovered and thereby not be random or a problem in the overall scheme of existence at all. Alternately, it could be posed (in the style of existential philosophies) that randomness and problems must be the result of a certain perspective, that one person's pattern is another person's chaos and that no one perspective holds the entire truth.[9] Even mathematics such as Ramsey's theorem or the weak Pinsker conjecture that demonstrate that given enough randomness, patterns will always arise seems to place randomness and determination as going hand in hand. However, from either of these positions, it becomes very tricky to rectify any meaning at all. For example, if on the one hand a pattern, a random occurrence or a problem are merely a perspective, then from which order do they derive in the first place? On the other hand, if all things have an order, they must therefore fit into one order or another, but from such a position thought or meaning lose their value without a contrast from which to distinguish them. This point can be developed in reference to Meilleassoux's (2009) work on 'Hume's problem'; i.e. how can we know that the laws of causality will continue in the future as they have done in the past? Meillassoux argues (on the extreme end of solutions to this problem) that we should take seriously the possibility that there is no necessity to causality which instead demonstrates an absolute necessity that the laws of nature to be contingent (which he contrasts against Hume's assertion of the necessity of causal connection).[10] His solution is developed in response to Kant's (2007) understanding of antimony and transcendence. Whereas Kant understands antimony as a contradiction arising whenever the thinker attempts to apprehend the nature of transcendent reality, and therefore represents something that cannot be known empirically. Meillassoux holds that it is an absurdity to be sure that you are unsure of an independent reality, as it would result in you being sure of something even if it is an uncertain reality. Therefore, for Meillassoux, antimony is rather the basis for knowing the modality of nature to be contingency. From both points of view, the infinite represents a contradiction, for Kant this contradiction represents an impossible point to think beyond, for Meillassoux this contradiction represents an impossibility in the laws of nature that implies contingency. Introducing the infinite middle position of meaning (presented by the method) leads to even deeper absurdities preventing either point of view from resolving the argument. To believe in contingency as the only necessity implies that existence is changeable, thereby neither absolutely conforming to a pattern or randomness. However, to imply contingency as a necessity implies a constant: that of contingency.[11] This, in turn, evokes a pattern which takes the argument back to the original position representable on the table above.

Beyond this point, only mathematics and not words can offer further meaningful expression on these laws. The profundity of this position can be seen in pi. The decimal positions of Pi are infinite and thought to never settle into a regular pattern, yet the number represents a constant for the ratio of a circle. Within pi is both an infinite (and constant) pattern and a problem, but it is only in the infinite that either the pattern or the problem fully emerges (other examples could be stochastic geometry or theories of tessellation). Therefore, the resolution of this problem is off access, and poses a limit to subjective thought and meaning, yet is also always inescapable and imminent at the same time. This gives an insight into the profundity of the contrast that underpins meaning; all things gain their properties from the ratio of that which opposes them, including thought and reflection. Objects on their own in themselves (without contrast) cannot be known, not because they are only an interpretation but because things do not exist without contrasting something else.[12] The same can also be said of ideals as the meaning of an ideal can only be derived from contrasting ideals. Thoughts and objects are each bound and characterised by this requirement; both objectivity and subjectivity must contrast.[13] Such viewpoints were foundational to both empiricism or rationalism as discussed by Descartes, Locke or Berkley, who all argued that objects must oppose ideas. According to all three, ideas must not be accessible to more than one sense, not presented to more than one observer, and not exist independently of being perceived (Ayer, 1991, chap. III). Therefore, contrast is needed for material to correspond with its nature. This point is made more tangible when considering the physical state of contrast itself; contrast is not isolatable or observable on its own, nor does it have any material attributes, yet it is indispensable to sense. The properties of contrasts are only perceivable from the materials or ideas used to make them, not the contrast itself. As such, contrast is the infinite (and excluded) middle of all things.

Attempting to resolve contrast initiates a question of scale getting infinitely bigger or smaller to encompass or absolve everything (or interiority verses exteriority as in Merleau-Ponty, 1964). It is unclear how small or large one must go to find an absolute zero devoid of anything at all, or to be able to count an absolute one that encompasses all matter, and a viewpoint beyond these limits from which to gain perspective. For example, when clapping your hands in which direction does the sound go? The only way to observe everything would be from a position of nothing, and nothing from a position of everything. The observation of each state would require an impossible perspective free of contrast. Instead, our perspective is more understandable a recursive relationship with that which it views. This can be demonstrated by Mandelbrot (2007) when asking 'How Long is the Coast of Britain?', the answer changes according to the scale of measurement used, an infinitely smaller measure would produce an infinite number of results. The answer as to whether it is possible to get an infinitely smaller scale is a genuine mystery as explained by Heisenberg's uncertainty principle. We cannot know if the world either on the smallest scale or the largest is in pattern or chaos. The concept of a pattern is highlighted against chaos and chaos against a pattern which could be seen to regressing into infinity (or oblivion). However, their meaning never lets this happen, as at the very midpoint between the two opposing concepts (such as patterns and chaos) a new concept is created (in this case the concept of a problem), which makes sense of the original two opposites. This means that rather than being infinitely regressive contrast is also infinitely abundant or productive. This infinity in meaning holds more than enough room for all conceptual forms to be contained. Perspective therefore, is not from a position of nothing or everything, but comes from a position of absolute contrast. This contrast both is and isn't relative; the relationship between the things contrasted is relative, but the actual contrast (un-scalable and infinite) used to make the distinction is absolute.

The implications of this unresolvable pattern can be found in the well-trod dualism of 'the problem of free will' or 'dilemma of determinism'.[14] More specifically, is thought doomed to be determined merely by the patterns of nature, or do these patterns allow for free will in some way? In keeping with the method proposed this contrast need not be resolved. Unlike idealism, contrast cannot be entirely aligned with will or reason, our will must be in contrast with contrast at all times. Will can therefore be argued to both conform to this infinite pattern, whilst also having the ability to make inferences on that pattern. Implying that all things share a predetermined destiny or fate, but one that contradictorily allows for choice. If it is possible to pick our truths in this way, it must be done so according to the truths possible, therefore affirming that all concepts are never wholly true or false. We get to make the worlds that we believe in (as espoused in the pragmatism of James) but must always accord those worlds around all others encountered. Therefore, freewill must always oppose something, and so whatever opposes our perspective will determine our fate as much as our own (including the perspectives of others). Existence must be in accordance with all things, including ourselves. The condition of subjectivity implies there to be both one truth common to us all as well as many individual perspectives that contradictorily don't add up to one common truth.

## Existence

This consistent focus on contrast becomes confusing when considering the exact vision of existence it is leading to. Is contrast one thing, two things, many things or not comprehendible as a thing in any way at all? Similarly, is the contrast itself homogenous or heterogeneous? An inexhaustible amount of philosophical positions can be taken in relation to contrast. All of the concepts presented by the method so far have conveyed deeper, interrelated meanings when contrasted. Confusingly, contrast has comprised the boundless source for all interpretation, yet on the other has imposed the source of all limits. If all of these concepts are related yet contradictory, how do they explain their own existence, or being? Heidegger used the term of ' the given', to argue that the idea of being is self-referent in every concept; if a concept can be used at all, it must imply its existence. Existence is implied by language, yet is also presented differently to the individuals, religions, sciences and philosophies that try to reflect on it. The question of agreeing on a universally accepted definition of existence is problematic, as existence can only be defined through actual being, which any definition is only ever in reference to. This point is implicit to Heidegger's (2013) use of Dasein (the existence of a subject) as distinct from the concept of existence in general (objective being). A point also central to much 20thC existential and post-structural philosophy. In Heidegger's distinction, the existence of a subject opposes objective existence. This makes subjective reflection on the concept of existence recessive. A subject cannot deny their existence but has no means to affirm any other perspective than their own.[15] The result is that the subject becomes overemphasised. To get beyond this regression requires a reconsideration of the relation of concepts to our sense of contrast. Contrasting concepts into a spectrum (as demonstrated by the method postulated), ends this regression by referring the concepts back to their original meanings. When collated into a spectrum, the perspective gained gives a glimpse of the concept aside from its subjective interpretation. The being of the concepts compiled, is as experienced through the individual, but also constitutes its own being written in the wider forces that govern meaning. The concept of existence forms the next concept spectrum below:

**Figure III-4**

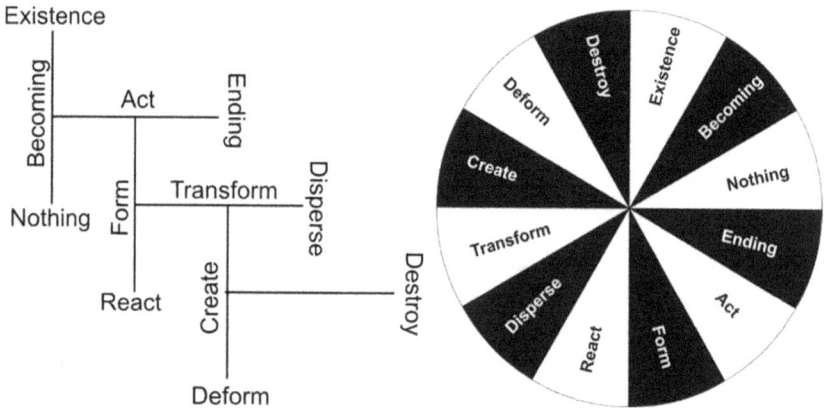

**Table III-4**

| Existence | Act | Disband |
|---|---|---|
| Existence is the concept of what's given or actual. | Between becoming and ending is to act, as acting is to evoke the becoming or ending of something. | The opposite of taking a form is to disband something altogether. |
| Nothingness |  | Transform |
| The opposite of being is nothingness. Nothingness is inherently challenging as its meaning must always oppose | React

Action is an extremely tricky concept as it is hard | Between forming and disbanding is to transform, to take a form |

| | | |
|---|---|---|
| existence. For Hegel, nothingness is the prerequisite of existence. However, here with the focus on meaning emanating from contrast it is not possible to reach this conclusion as contrast does not exist in nothingness alone, it always relies upon something else. Therefore, our only recourse for understanding the concept is as the total opposition to existence. | to imagine it's opposite. Is it ever possible not to act as not acting also constitutes an action. For this reason, actions opposite must be a reaction as it is to act on the original action. (The whole world could be considered in this cycle, as the reaction to an action. But there must be action otherwise what would create the reaction?). | and to form it into something else entirely. Deform The opposite of transformation is to deform something, to take a form and then leave the constituent parts behind. |
| Becoming Between being and nothing is becoming, the course all things are going through. Becoming is the sense of something going from something to something. Such a concept has very ancient roots in philosophy (as in Heraclitus or i-ching). | Form Between action and reaction is the taking of a form, as a form is the result of acting or reacting. This concept could also be described as making a boundary to things. | Destroy Between transformation and deformation is destruction as destruction is common to both practices. Create |
| Ending The opposite to becoming is ending. This is to put a boundary (or form) on something and denote that it is no longer able to change. This means that to declare something has ended can be political or contested. | | The opposite of destruction is creation, to bring something into being. Which brings us back to the concept of existence. Existence is that which is present between creation and destruction. |

Each of these concepts on their own could be considered as a mode of existence. As a result, when combined they pose a range of competing contrasts. This poses a dilemma as no single concept on this wheel is absolute or exists in isolation from the others. Conversely, attempting to take a position that attempts to encompass as many of the contradictions as possible nullifies the profundity of the meaning between these contradictions. In this way, existence can only be reflected upon by concepts that are partial to their own existence. Just as the meaning of concepts are impossible to express in their entirety at any one time, the same must be true for the meaning of existence. Similarly, to express the profoundness of being through logic, would require the impossible task of making all things logically compatible. Every time something is made logical, it is necessarily set aside from and made distinct from the illogical. Attempting to render the whole of existence as logical always requires excluding other versions of the universe as illogical and therefore be partial (as seen in set theory when confronting 'Russell's paradox' Russell, 1967). This implies that the task of making logic is fixed as a cycle of inclusions that always implies something else (like Sisyphus' never-ending task of rolling a bolder up a hill only for the bolder to escape when nearing the top).

The table above attempts to represent the order of all things. However, it can only approach the subject through a range of contradictions. Consequently, what is represented offers a glimpse of the limits of conceptualisation. It demonstrates at its most fundamental the gap between observation and representation. The concept most elemental able to demonstrate these contrasts is that of observable energy. Aristotle's (1998) original concept of enérgeia was defined as 'being at work'. The modern meaning of the concept deviates from its etymology through its close associated with the development of scientific methodologies and attachment to some of the major principles in science (E.g. the conservation of energy or E=MC2). The thrust of scientific method has sought to find ways in which the concept can be observed as a consistent unit (e.g. a Watt a Joule or Kelvin). As a result, it is often at odds with modern usages of energy and opposed to any pre-existing 'metaphysical' implications of the word that may confuse these principles. Aside from these contestations however, even at the abstract scientific level, energy is notoriously difficult to define, and as with Aristotle's original assertion that energy can only be made clear by looking at examples rather than trying to find a definition, modern sciences understanding of energy also crucially hinges upon never venturing beyond explanations of energy as observed and manifest (most evident in science education's approach to the concept of energy). This results in an understanding of energy as closely related to, and merely a different form of matter.

To view energy as only ever seen through its effects on matter with no other physical presence implies that energy must be opposed to matter, and that physical objects are impossible with no energy and vice versa (as in the Bose-Einstein condensate or in total entropy all things without energy or with uniform energy become one and therefore indistinguishable from everything and nothing). Therefore, calculating energy as opposition i.e. E=MC2, has led to the vast array of scientific knowledge of the standard model that unitises particles and energy into a series of constituent parts (even if some famous scientific inconsistencies still remain incompatible e.g. gravity or baryon asymmetry). During the same period, the biggest questions raised in philosophy ask how these forms equate to experience especially in language (as raised in existentialist philosophies, post-structuralism and to some extent analytic philosophy). The result of much of this has been an over-emphasis on the incommensurability of the subjective and objective (the latest iterations of such debates in speculative realism acknowledge the certainty of an existence larger than the subject but emphasis how this demonstrates the limits of human subjects to ever know it entirely). As much of these issues remain unresolved the question remains, at what point do the states observed in science separate into distinguishable units rather than be one immense state, and at what point exactly are the two states distinguishable from one another. As has been seen (in the problem of scale), it is difficult to say with absolute certainty at what point one thing starts or ends without contrast. Even quantum superposition (according to the Copenhagen Interpretation and Heisenberg's uncertainty principle) dictates that the position of atomic particles are impossible to place in one single space or time.[16] This means it is impossible to state with absolute accuracy, when or where one thing becomes another or the point where energy transfers or transforms. Therefore, in all of these deductions both scientific or philosophical, the only thing certain is that to be knowable, things must contrast that which they are not. But how can such a contrast be pinpointed?

The physical can only be encountered as contrasted, but otherwise, contrast is unaccountable, and in this sense means contrast is metaphysical.[17] Any presence can only be experienced as a sense of contrasts. These senses all present as distinct physical things however, contrast can only be understood through reflection i.e. actions and equal and opposite reactions. Such reflections are evidence of a cycle, without energy matter would have no form, but without matter energy would have no medium. Neither one of them alone create contrast, both are required. The contrast is not matter or energy it is whatever is between the two causing things to be opposed to each other, the infinite regress of scale (i.e. the thing behind the Pauli Exclusion Principle). Therefore, contrast must be totally opposed to both matter and energy. Or to use the terminology of physics, both in and beyond spacetime and infinitely opposing both energy and matter exactly at the point where they meet. This infinite contrast must be in perfect symmetry and as it occupies an ambiguous space and time could be said to be both infinitely recurrent, and static, as well as implying both immensity, as well as minutiae. Contrast is always presented as both extremely specific and localised as well as inexhaustive and universal.[18] This explains the loops found here in meaning (or the symmetry of musical notes, or colours) as they can be interpreted as never-ending as well as regulated into specific patterned meanings.

Thinking about contrast in this way initiates a peculiar philosophical stance. It firstly links thought to material by demonstrating contrast as a required condition for the experience of either, but in so doing must necessarily acknowledge that all worldviews have some truth whilst no one worldview can demonstrate truth entirely. For example, existence can be demonstrated as a monism (i.e. all things derive from one, often considered the first philosophical digression by Parmenides via Plato, 1996) or its exact opposite at the same time, a dualism (consciousness represents something inherently different to the physical world), or a state which opposes both, a pluralism/multiplicity (a state where more than one condition coexist, first illustrated by Heraclitus' and dialecticisms unity of opposites contrasting Parmenides). Similarly, the structure of existence is impossible to define absolutely as it must be linear, as well as cyclical, stratified, homogeneous or heterogeneous, dependant on where the boundaries are drawn. Such a paradox is presented to us as infinity, as one thing yet also many. This could be said to imply the inability of concepts to represent reality, as argued, however, the problem more closely resembles logical reductionism (logocentrism) as concepts are just as much reality as the things they represent. As such, concepts must be as ambiguous as to where they begin or end, and be as simultaneously singular and multi-modal as the realities they represent. The ways in which one accords as well as disaccords the other is to be expected therefore, as it is in the same way as all other things. All concepts exist in relation to all other concepts, and when charted each perspective has a symmetry towards the whole of existence. Therefore, existence is confusingly all things with no exclusions as well as being no things with all exclusions.

## Contrast

This method has repeatedly uncovered contrast as essential to all meaning. This implies that contrast must pre-empt all of the concepts demonstrated as well as be reliant on them for expression. However, in as much as meaning is derived from contrast, it must also be the point at which meaning becomes meaningless. Therefore, contrast itself offers an impasse as it is both meaningful and not meaningful, absolute and conditional at the same time. Contrast can be seen to oppose its own conceptualisation (just as it opposes matter and energy). This opposition accompanies contrast each time it is given a name, as the experience of contrast is always wider than the name, and therefore necessarily generates a whole language to compensate. Unlike concepts, contrast can be considered both relational and not at the same time. Contrast goes beyond what is observable unto meaninglessness, yet can only be found in relation to something else. The point where any one thing contrasts another (which is always infinite) marks where that things meaning is distinguishable from everything else. This has big implication for ideals as the experience of contrast blurs the line between subjective, internal experience and the world external to it. The sense of contrast must be both internal and external at the same time. To understand this position better requires charting the concept of contrast itself:

## Figure III-5

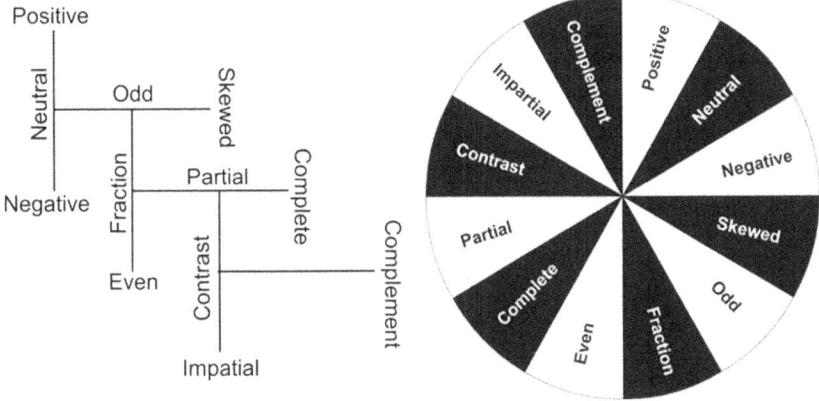

## Table III-5

| Positive | Even | Impartiality |
|---|---|---|
| Positive is one part of a larger polarised entity or grouping (positive/negative are difficult to conceptualise as they are indirect concepts that only exist in reference to something else). | Between neutral and biased is the concept of something being even, this means that all constituent parts add up to something that can be halved without a fracture. | Between a fraction and completion is something that is impartial, meaning that fractions and completion are to be regarded as equal. |
| Negative | Odd | Partiality |
| Negative is the opposite occupant of the same larger polarised entity or grouping. | The opposite of something even is something odd, which means something which cannot be halved into equal constituent parts. | The opposite of impartiality is partiality, which is that which is on its own from its surroundings. This implies a larger entity that is made up of smaller parts. This conception has its ultimate expression at the level of the whole universe and our being as the parts within it. |
| Neutral | Fraction | Contrast |
| Neutrality is the point exactly between positive and negative, and refers to something with equal constituents parts that make its overall. | Between even and odd is a fraction, which refers to the remainder of an entity that once divided does not constitute a whole. | Contrast is between partiality and impartiality and is when something is both part of something whilst also being apart. It is the exception to all things that also forms a rule. |
| Biased | Completion | Complimentary |
| The concept of bias is the opposite of neutrality and | Completion is the opposite of a fraction. That which is | The opposite of a contrast is a complement, which is when a part |

| refers to something that is constituted with unequal parts. | complete is something that is a whole entity of and in itself. | resonates with a part of something else. It is the rule to all things that must remain an exception. |

These concepts describe a series of counterpoints which defines how objects are positioned against their surroundings. As a result, all of these concepts are a variance on contrast in some way, however, none of which (including the concept of contrast) can be said to be the one true and total representation of contrast as experienced. Contrast is present in all relations including neutrality. This restricts an imagination of their being some neutral cosmic backdrop to existence from which to base reality and the nature of things in themselves. Each state relies on contrast to another to exert its being. This makes contrast all the more peculiar. To consider contrast as always between two things results in it being ambiguous as to whether it is objective or subjective (a noumena or a phenomena) and as to where exactly it can be located. Contrast cannot be something physical like a substance or matter. Otherwise, where would it accumulate or go to? So contrast must be as non-physical (or metaphysical) as it is physical. This might imply that without an observer there can be no contrast. However, if energy and matter are contrasting, the world outside consciousness just like inside of consciousness must abound with contrast. Therefore, contrast must be both objective and subjective. This means that consciousness must be configured in some way around this incongruity, and therefore knowing consciousness is linked to the interpretation of contrast.

The 'hard problem' introduced to neuroscience by David Chalmers (1995) argues that the instruments developed to look at the activities of nerves and neurons can see the structures of the neurons and can measure the electrical activity as it moves through cerebral networks but finds it hard to equate the data or models generated to the experience of consciousness. Contrast could be said to suffer from a similar problem. Contrast is present in every measurement, but there can be no way to measure it aside from its physical attributes. This can be compared to consciousness. As contrast is located in the reaction between energy and matter, neither fully being either energy or matter, in the same way, consciousness could be suspended between the material (i.e. neurons etc.) and the energies (electromagnetic, chemical) that are active with the brain and intermediate with it. In this sense, consciousness (sense or feeling) would not be the material of the brain or the energy that moves through it, but located between the two at the moment energy and matter transforms. A good way to imagine this link between experience and contrast is through colour. Colour is said to only exist as a sensual experience, as the result of refraction in white light. In that same way, meaning could be said to be the sensual experience of the appreciation of the contrast between mental matter and energy. Just as with contrast, consciousness occupies an ambiguous place in space and time as to attempt to discover the exact place energy meets brain matter evokes an infinite scale (such possibilities are explored, but not resolved in the hubris of wave function collapse).

A subject surrounded in every sense by a wider universe must only ever be in a position of contrast. As such, the question is not where the individual stops and the universe begins, rather understanding the contrast that gives both definition. If consciousness occurs between the energy, nerves and neurons it would be reductive to neither. This makes consciousness different to both material and energy yet operating on the same standard. Thought echoes the patterns observable in physics, but as a reflection would not be entirely reducible to physics, and so retain both naturalistic and idealistic characteristics at the same time.[19] Consciousness shares an existence in common with all things observable, whilst always representing something more. The regulation of thoughts or feelings emanates from the contrasts observable between energy and matter. This explains why it is difficult to reflect on consciousness with consciousness, as such a reflection is always from a position of contrast and so only ever in reflection. Such a reflection is hindered to reflect experience inwardly and the wider world outwardly. The reflection from within such a contrast is infinite in scale. However, one of the most fundamental experiences of being is the appreciation of the finite. Therefore, a prerequisite of consciousness is the simultaneous appreciation of finite situatedness as well as the infinity between. Just as psychoanalysis is foundered upon the unconscious, the dynamic of contrast between situatedness and infinite reflection can be compared to that of the conscious and subconscious (especially evocative of Jung's 2014 'collective unconscious', which places the unconscious away from the ego or self, and Freud's 2003 concept of the uncanny as familiar yet unfamiliar). This opens up to interpretation the space and expanse available to the mind. An infinite chaotic space that can, at the same time, be organised into a pattern. On to this situated infinity, analysis can project countless distinctions, like Bergson's (2014) qualitative multiplicity, but ultimately consciousness (as meaning) is always more than the sum of its parts and escapes any one definition.[20] This quality is essential for thought to be able to think within the world surrounding it.

As a result, the appreciation of opposition encompasses one of the profoundest of experiences for life. As contrast is used to distinguish concepts, no single concept alone can encompass this sensation, for example at a certain level opposition is impossible to tell if complimentary or contrasting, which incidentally constitutes both the meaning of opposition and symmetry. Likewise, all things associated as being senses (logic, emotion) must be engaged with appreciating opposition. In this way opposition can be understood in comparison to a rhyme. Rhyme constitutes a meaning on a meaning, i.e. a literal meaning and meaning occurring from the correspondence of sounds, therefore rhyme has a double meaning. The appreciation of a rhyme comes from the aligning of two senses appreciating oppositions at the same time (also evident in appreciation of complementary colours or musical notes). Meaning, therefore, is felt as contrast and arranged around oppositions, whether it's in the form of a taste, touch, sight, smell, or sound (and to this other semi and non-perceptive senses can be considered), thought and emotion align these senses into a coherent (and symmetrical) structure.[21] Intelligence is the mastering of bringing these sensations together in coherent overarching distinct opposites that juxtapose into a narrative. But just as any act of intelligence organises opposition together, something always escapes as once any narrative is created, at the same time an opposing schema is also made possible. Therefore, all intelligence from distinguishing basic objects to the great works of music, art, maths, science and humanities must be engaged with the same task of arranging contrast over multiple oppositions.

**Table III-6**

---

**Chapter Summary:**
- Meaning is contrasted against matter.
- The sensation of contrast is one of infinite bounds, however, any single expression of this sensation can never represent this infinity in its entirety.
- Narrative is a means to link what would otherwise be contradictory into a coherent structure.
- Neutrality may not be considered as absolute, i.e. we have no access to neutrality without something with which to contrast it against, and therefore we have no basis with which to consider an all-encompassing neutralising state acting as a backdrop for all existence, just as the laws of nature cannot be described as an absolute contingency or absolute causality alone.
- Perspective must always assume a place between itself and that which it reflects.

---

# Endnotes

[1] My account seeks an understanding of meaning that is as encompassing as possible. As a result, it is a non-linguistic theory of meaning, or a theory of meaning that attempts to pre-figure linguistic meaning. More specific examples could be, in verificationist theories of meaning such as proposed by Carnap or Wittgenstein, which hold that meaning must be verified by experience, my view of contrast is that it can be interpreted as both experiential and contrasted against it. Or in reference to the causal theory of reference developed by Putnam or Kripke which holds that terms acquire specific referents based on evidence, the account here diverts the attention from discussions around referents being internal or external to the mind, by demonstrating contrasts as both internal and external.

A similar consideration can be aimed towards continental style semiotics, by using opposition to confuse the relationship between sign and signifier.

2 This example could be expanded by considering how mathematics and physics speculates on extra dimensions from the work of Theodor Kaluza to string theory. The concept of nothingness as unlimited requires ever more dimensions to fill the void in explanation of what is constituting the nothingness. Without an explanation of how all observable physical forces are unified this speculation is perpetuated.

3 This point could be developed using studies that emphasise how communication is not specifically sited in one place but embodied or integrated between consciousness and experience. These point are followed in the communicology of Laignan (2010). Also see Butchart (2019) and Catt (2014).

4 The argument here is not intending to perpetuate the same polarised argument as that tread between Chomsky and Foucault on the possibility (and impossibility) of a universal grammar. Rather than the object here being the innate structures of human thinking or understanding, instead it is to look at the dynamics of thought as contrasting. This means that it is impossible for us to get a gods eye view of thought outside of our own perspective. Rather than resolve the debate around universal grammar, or innate human experience I wish to argue that a meaning that is unrelated to another meanings is impossible to think, which provides the basis for us to argue that language can be both innate and not at the same time and so continually perpetuates the relevance of the question.

5 The word disenchantment comes via Friedrich Schiller. This theme was seen as significant in the modern period, also see Frazer's (2009) theory of the three stages of human belief published in 1890, which argued that beliefs went from primitive magic, to religion and then science.

6 Making the line between process philosophy, object oriented ontology and speculative realism confusing to navigate.

7 Also see, authors like Haraway who bemoans this as the 'gods eye view from nowhere'. Or Adorno & Horkheimer see the fact that every perspective is narrative as resulting in a bleak spectre which emphasizes human limitation and the unassailability between thought and the worlds it inhabits.

8 The opposite concept to pattern is tricky to pin down, here I align the sense of the meaning of this concept with chaos or haphazardness but could be linked with randomness or determinism. The concept of chance can also be associated with the spectrum the absolute which again highlights the tricky conceptualisation of the absolute, as randomness here only exists in relation to its opposite pattern and not an absolute.

9 Or perhaps in the style of Koyre (2016), one epochs fixed stars are another's infinite universe.

10 Some interpretations of Hegel would argue that Hegel already argues for the absolute necessity of contingency, see Zantvoort (2015).

11 This would imply therefore that we can neither affirm or disaffirm transcendence or contingency as our perspective is always between their meanings, highlighting the durability of Kant's legacy (see Clemens, 2013; Malabou, 2016).

[12] Compared to object-orientated ontology (see Harman, 2011), this point can be seen to both overmine and undermine objects, the preservation of finitude and non-exhaustion of objects is not upheld. Rather objects are only gain these properties through contrast.

[13] This is demonstrable when questioning the existence of numbers (see the synthetic philosophy of mathematics Zalamea, 2019). Numbers are ideals that can never be represented absolutely in material, whilst the accuracy of arithmetic points to something verifiable beyond the individual (this corresponds to the difficult to resolve debates in the philosophy of mathematics of Platonism, nominalism or fictionalism).

[14] Explored in the work of Galen Strawson (2010).

[15] Generally developed since Nietzsche. Derrida's (2016) deconstruction offered a method to abstract and view the limits of subjective meaning and challenge logocentrism, which was to the ire of analytic philosophers such as Quine. But proved a victim of its own success in not offering a further recourse for interpretations other than through further perspectivisms. At all times something opposing perspective is undeniable, and so perspectivism must rely on its opposite for meaning, making it just as valid as any other perspective. And meaning that perspective affirms something bigger than it.

[16] Karen Barad's (2007) agential realism has developed what this indeterminacy may be for matter and meaning.

[17] This complements as much as contradicts Heidegger's reservations with Cartesianism, in the sense that being as experienced and being as thought are a necessary contradiction. And therefore to say that there is no such thing as metaphysics only one thing is a matter of perspective.

[18] This understanding of contrast could be used to imply transcendentalism as in Kant's use of the term. However, as contrast is always intimately connected to contrast it could also be taken to contradict it.

[19] Naturalism or physicalism as propounded by Dennett (2007) or Quine (and many related fields exist to following these examples) and has many implications for the study of consciousness as it makes the assumption to link consciousness to 'natural process'. As has been pointed out this process is partial as it assumes physics before consciousness. Such an understanding of consciousness could also be completely inverted to imply that extreme opposite, that the entirety of nature is one big thought process thereby annulling any claims to materialism at all, such as Kastrup (2019).

[20] For example theories such as Giulio Tononi's (2014) Integrated Information Theory can demonstrate that the brain conveys high levels of integrated information, or Bernard Baars' (1988) Global Workspace Theory can demonstrate how messages are broadcast in the brain, or Francis Crick and Christof Koch (1990) have demonstrated that the brain generates 40-hertz oscillations. All these theories however lack explanation of accounting for and demonstrating the experience of consciousness and what actually constitutes it.

[21] Theories of autopoiesis such as that of Maturana and Varela (1979) demonstrate some of these observations by suggesting a model of cognition where nervous and higher brain functions are cyclical and each fulfil the necessity of the other. A more modern version of these arguments can also be found in Hui (2019). This doesn't explain what is behind the cycle however, and why these functions would become cyclical in the first place.

Chapter IV

# Consequence

*"It is the burden of life to be many ages without seeing the end of time"*
(Jim Harrison)

The last section used the rhetoric/dialectic method to explore how meaning and being are related to contrast. Contrast cannot be fully placed either in our sense of the world, or beyond us in existence as observed. Rather contrast is entirely uncertain as to whether it is physical or not. The implication for such a move opens up an ambiguous space for a metaphysics which is not so much at odds with physics and the natural sciences (closed down by post-enlightenment philosophy). Consequently, the major themes of idealism (Spirit, Will or Life) as well as what traditionally opposes them come into contact (albeit while relegating idealisms claim to absolution). If meaning is placed in the contrast between matter, unobserved contrast cannot alter substance at will, it is only through some notion of sentience that contrast can be made meaningful, distinct and positioned. Therefore, the final section will explore what contrast means to be alive, human and an individual and to be engaged with making distinctions, using the concepts of life; mind; the human and society to do this.

## Life

If sensation and consciousness can be linked to contrast, what does this imply for the ways in which life is understood. Enlightenment philosophy used the concept of sentience to distinguish organisms that could feel from those that could reason as a way to define thought as distinct from a wider notion of life. As a result, the modern meaning of life is entwined with the meanings of consciousness and sensation, but with a blurred sense of where these lines meet. The problem leads to conflicting visions of life as either varying in levels, increasing with the sophistication of reflection, or as a constant independent of cognition (a good demonstration of this history can be found in Schrodinger, 2012 written in 1944). In this sense life is a loaded concept, biased by sentient beings. However, without the concept of life distinguishing subjects or objects (whether living or not) from their surroundings becomes difficult, as without life what would be the force responsible for making the distinction in the first place? In this way, life must be common to observable physical substances, whilst being opposed to physics at the same time. The part of substance that remains omnipresent yet ephemeral through all physical transformations. This is represented in philosophy by the problem of dualism vs. pansychism. Panpsychism is the assertion that sentience is common to the physical world (for example see Strawson's 2006 stance on dual-aspect monism),[1] whilst dualism is to assert that life is somehow separate and apart from the physical world (as in Cartesianism discussed further below). But rather than wholly conforming to dualism or panpsychism's monism what is highlighted (by the method postulated) is its partial truth and fallacy, as on the one hand consciousness and sensation (linked to life) are linked to contrast which also occurs between matter and energy, but on the other hand, physics must be distinct from feeling or life wouldn't be able to appreciate it? For example, contrast can be felt by the subject, but one subject may never directly feel another subject's life (only contrast). Therefore, the approach here is as reminiscent of a panpsychism as it is of (its antithesis) dualism. Just as the contrast is located in the interaction between energy and matter, life must be located in things capable of sensing contrast. In this sense life is not a thing, it's a ratio. Section IV will therefore put forwards how the method postulated can accommodate all distinctions of sentience, e.g. life and consciousness from physical matter and energy, as well as distinguishing between the different indicators of sentience, e.g. life, mind, body, human, animal, etc. What I wish to demonstrate is that sentience and life are familiar to, yet distinct from their constituent parts. This leads to a consideration of life as common to the manifestations of observable physics but also wholly apart (rather it occupies the infinite contrast between observations). Life must be understood both as its own distinct thing otherwise it could not make sense to itself, and life would have no meaning, but it must also exist in relation to the conditions surrounding it within which it exists:

**Figure IV-1**

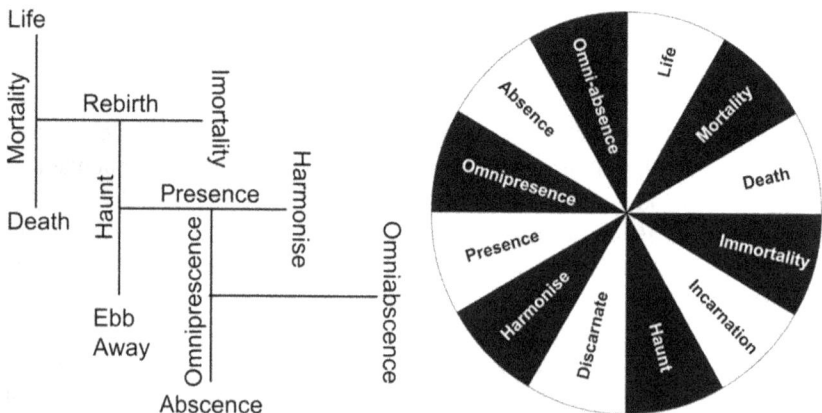

**Table IV-1**

| Life | Incarnation | Presence |
|---|---|---|
| Life occupies an ambiguous presence materially. From this ambiguity life can appreciate energy independent of material: i.e. it is that which is sentient. | Incarnation is the state of something going from non-existence to life. This could be considered as a very specific event in an individual's life but when viewed in a broader sense is also what happens to the material of our bodies on a constant basis. All life is in the process of giving way to new life. | Between haunt and harmonise, presence is the state of being somewhere. |
| **Death** | | **Absence** |
| Life's opposite of death, therefore, is the depreciation of energy-dependent on material. | **Reincarnation** The opposite of incarnation is for an entity to be reincarnated. Reincarnation is not the beginning of new subjects but a new beginning. | Opposite to presence absence is the state of not being somewhere (presence and absence are very similar to being and nothingness, the major difference being the positioning of the subject, absence and presence imply the subject to be positioned in a space relative to others). |
| **Mortality** Between life and death is the state of being mortal. Something that is in the process of demise. | **Haunt/Enchant** Between birth and rebirth is to haunt, to not be fully born or reborn, but to stay behind in some way.[2] One strong example of this could be in the memories and folk laws of others, or the uncanny. | **Omnipresent** Between presence and absence omnipresence is the state of both being somewhere and nowhere at the same time. |
| **Immortality** Immortality is presence beyond life and death. Something that has no demise. | **Harmonise/Disenchant** To harmonise is the opposite of haunt in that it offers an example to others that brings believers into line with each other. | **Separate** The opposite of omnipresence would entail being separate in a state of isolation or omni-absence. Which leads back to life, those living sense beyond their immediate surroundings whilst also always being situated, occupying an ambiguous presence between body and environment. |

To understand the method postulated, meaning, sentience, life and consciousness must be placed in the contrast that is between things rather than in the things themselves, however, as soon as life is thought it is objectified and ceases to align with contrast and instead its place is akin to all other objects. Therefore, life shares an affinity with contrast but no one thought can ever contain or encapsulate all its meaning as contrast is ever-changing. In this regard, life occupies a very similar position as death and each one is reliant on the other for meaning. Life's reliance on death means that life cannot be consciousness or sensation alone or it would sustain no form with which to distinguish contrast against (for Rank, 1998 and; Becker, 1985 death makes life meaningful). This leads to a contradiction, life is reliant upon a situated, temporal physical form with which to reside (a body), whilst at the same time only ever occupying the contrast between physical things. As such the body's temporality and situatedness also makes death inevitable, and means that life is never far from death. Without death, life and the major themes of life (e.g. loss, hope, love, fulfilment) would be unthinkable. Reflection of our own inevitable death constitutes one of the biggest contradictions of experience, when considering that what exists beyond the position a subject is used to make the meaning. One of the biggest profundities of thought is the fact that death can be speculated on at all (a so-called negative existential), as when one speculates on death they are only ever really doing it through life (Ariès, 1982). Yet there must be some beyond, for if there wasn't there would be no reaction (or contrast) between energy and matter or force with which to make distinctions. The ultimate death therefore, is the death of contrast (absolute entropy), i.e. becoming indistinguishable from the world around ("the cancelling of difference" Deleuze, 2014).

If life's most distinguishing feature is its appreciation of the subject, existence devoid of life could only ever be being with no real appreciation of difference (which would be the same as nothingness). However, as life exists, existence cannot slip into total ambiguity. In some way, the imprint of life illuminates whatever else life is not into meaningful existence (This is not to contradict Meillassoux 2009 who holds that death is a necessary proof of existence outside of thought). The concept of life is as undeniable as the subject as it predetermines thought, and through life, the subject can appreciate the whole loop of creation and its opposite. In this way the meaningfulness of life, experience and reality can be understood as the result of a pattern between energy and matter, however at the same time life must be reliant upon all things that exist as well as all things which oppose existence (and so neither monist, dualist or pluralist explanations of existence can ever be complete without each other). The extreme end of either possibility; existence devoid of opposition; or the totality of whatever opposes existence offers a natural limit as both extremes are devoid of distinction and therefore analogous with nothingness. Therefore, thought is integrally linked to the nothingness which is beyond the limits of what can be imagined, as nothingness initiates thoughts formulation and represents what thoughts returns back to once a thought is thought. Negative existentials are envisaged here as productive rather than paradoxical, i.e. negation or neutrality are not to be considered absolute as they always imply a value. This is to say that existence is not to be imagined as some perfect neutralised state beyond the individual for which we are striving to achieve. In order to achieve this, thought requires both the experience of positionality and an ambiguous position within that positionality. The distinction of life is therefore necessary, as life is not entirely thought, and not entirely the body which contains it. Life is on the frequency of this manifestation between being and its opposite. For example, consider the sunflower which radiates its seeds in golden mean, in Fibonacci sequence at its centre. Is it enacting some ideal ratio which appreciates the infinite to perform such a task or is it being guided by some infinite ideal on a path of least resistance? Ultimately, both eventualities imply the same thing, that being is ideal yet contrasted to ideals at the same time. Life makes visible a universal pattern that combines being and the contrast of it. In this sense, life and thought are the most potent defilement of nothingness (which is in itself also impossible to say whether only ideal or not), and with life's very existence nothingness is transformed, yet at the same time, the nothingness is essential to the constitution of thought and impossible without it.

In this way, life conforms to a pattern which it is also sworn to confound, regardless of how any one particular life is conducted. The sunflower can never achieve a perfect spiral as such a feat would need to be perfect in infinite scale, yet it is from the infinite that it has shaped its form. The thought of life as alternating between a pattern amongst the limitlessness of all patterns available at once evokes the sublime. Attempting to understand this pattern (against what it opposes) ultimately underlies the experience of subject-hood, and all life at varying stages of awareness must take part in some way. The same pattern can be portrayed contradictorily as absolute or relational, or used to imply divine meaning or nihilism. The result inadvertently and inescapably implies the need for both freewill, determinism and belief (of which we will use as the backdrop to the section).

## Mind and Body

The rhetoric/dialectic of life puts into stark contrast the limited positionality of the subject against the universality possible in thought. The most traditional version of this enquiry in western philosophy comes in the form of body contrasted against mind as found in Cartesianism (Descartes, 2008 following developments in optics by Kepler). The famous first principle of Cartaseanism, 'cogito, ergo sum' implies the existence of thought as a proof of the existence of the thinker. This principle sets in motion a distinction between the subject and object that has echoed through philosophy through the centuries since. Revered as much as condemned, the result of Cartesianism fragments knowledge into mind on the one hand and body on the other. By placing the mind as possible to achieve truth contrasted against the body (and the world around) for which we cannot be certain. Perhaps no dualism has had as much attention as mind and body and is consistently repeated because of the difficulty of refuting cogito. Cited as responsible for initiating the tradition of the search for absolute reason in philosophy, within Cartesian thought is the anxiety[3] of conforming the 'human' to reliable categorisation (which continues to be attempted in philosophical form such as naturalism, see Dennett, 2007). Since Heidegger, continental accounts have questioned the partiality to human experience and being implied by this split, but successive movements have struggled to avoid its influence.

Similarly, the method of dialectic/rhetoric postulated in this account is obliged to maintain as much as refute the Cartesian dualism. For example, the method cannot deny having a first principle or absolute, as the assertion that there is no one first principle or absolute alone, acts as a first principle. The method does offer a complexification, however; by focusing on the contrast from which reflexive thought derives, the method connects the contrast sensed in individual reflection of the subject to the contrast observed in any reflection upon objects beyond the individual. As a result, the method enables a perspective that distorts the subject/object distinction, contradictorily both unifying the distinctions whilst maintaining them as distinct. In this way, the method prompts a way to see the contradiction of the dualism as both productive and reductive. Therefore, reflecting on the mind-body dualism using the method postulated will help to gain a perspective on ways of thinking developed from and still tied to the Cartesian dualism to present how it is particular to western thought:

**Figure IV-2**

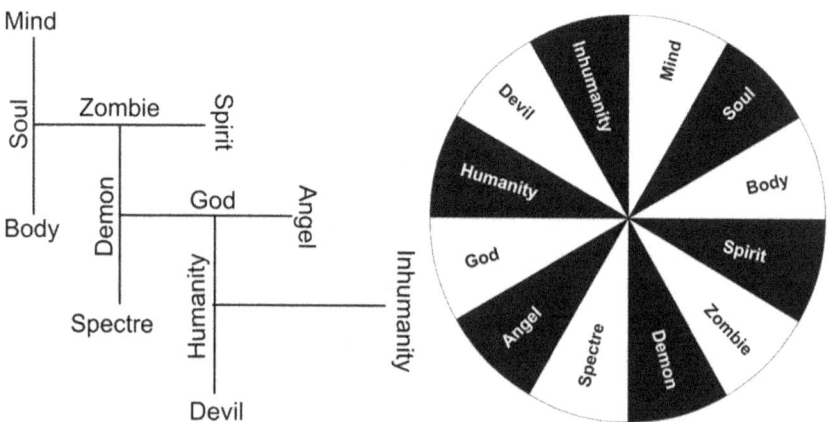

**Table IV-2**

| Mind | Zombie | God |
|---|---|---|
| According to Cartesian logic, the mind is that which cannot be denied to the thinker.

Body

Therefore, its opposite is that which it is possible to deny but which always remains present; the body.

Soul

Between mind and body is the entity that links both body and mind and defines the personal characteristics of an individual.

Spirit

The opposite of the soul therefore is a concept of spirit as governing the impersonal, universal, heavenly component of a human being (Spengler upholds this division and argues that it has been an essential characteristic to the development of the west).[4] | Between the soul and spirit is to imagine a human body without a human soul or spirit, which can be termed as a zombie, but may vary to different cultures in connotation.[5] (I had considered putting vampire here instead, as vampire is a body without a soul, and the category therefore is very similar whilst also used as a metaphor for capitalism).

Spectre

The opposite of a zombie is soul or spirit without a body. I have chosen to use the word spectre as this word may encompass very broadly the remnants of spirit that lingers on in some aspect.

Demon

Between a zombie and a spectre lies something inhuman, which is an adverse version of humanity. This needed be termed a demon and may be compared to other culturally adverse versions of inhumanity.

Angel

The opposite of an adverse form of humanity is an idealised form of humanity which can be conceptualised as an angel. But may also be compared to any idealised version of humanity. | Between the demons and angels is god which symbolises the ultimate force that accounts for the existence of humanity.

Devil

The opposite of god is the devil which represents existence at it most hostile to humanity.

Humanity

Between god and the devil is the concept of humanity which is the concept that there exists a condition which is agreeable to all humankind.

Inhumanity

The opposite of humanity is inhumanity, the concept of something being universally disagreeable to all humankind. Which brings us back to the mind, which has the ultimate power to decipher, define and work out the conditions of humanity. |

The resulting spectrum above demonstrates a series of peculiar tropes in western literature and culture (e.g. zombies, angels, demons, gods, devils, etc.). To argue that the meaning of mind and body are related to such fictitious concepts may stretch the limits of credibility and threaten to impinge on the rationality of the underlying concepts. However, rather than emphasise mind or body as fictional or constructed (any more than any other concept), I wish to argue that it can be used to highlight the highly positional, anthrocentric nature of taking mind alone as truth. Contrasting mind with body results in a non-holistic fracturation of humanity into its constituent parts. In this model, some bodily facets like emotion become very difficult to place in the ways introduced in the first chapter, for example, are emotions part of the mind or the body? Do emotions have any intelligence or first principle different to rationality of their own? The concept of a 'first principle' enshrines logic as supreme at the expense of a broader understanding of human experience, for example, things can be experienced emotionally that cannot be understood logically and vice versa. The only solution to which is to decentre rationality as the preeminent and principle form of all truths. First principles assume concepts are reaching towards coherence or wholeness, rather than accept the wholeness and coherence they already inherently have, neither being inherently right or wrong. This point is already referenced in Jung on Nietzsche: 'The body is merely the visibility of the soul, the psyche; and the soul is the psychological experience of the body. Soul and body are not two things they are really one' (Jung, 1988, p. 335). The renewed emphasis I am attempting to introduce however, is the consequence of emphasising any approach to the duality, regardless of whether in reference to the unity or separation of mind and body. Of chief concern is that any discussion of it skews consequent interpretations of existence by placing humanity at its centre.[6] In accordance with the growing influences of biocentric post-humanist studies, Cartesianism is conflated by questions such as: where does your mind stop and the exterior world begin; which parts of your mind are integral to it and separate to the world around them; and how can experiences of your mind be collated and differentiated from one mind to another? These questions are difficult to resolve with a rationalist first principle, as they demand an irrational (i.e. contradictory) solution. E.g. that the only thing which differentiates to the thinker their thought from the wider world is the contrast felt in that thought to inform the thinker that their thought is a reflection.

Therefore, the results confer that the Cartesian emphasis on mind, rationality and the human are a partial western interpretation of existence.[7] This conclusion is very similar to the major concerns of continental thought since the 20th century, such as post-structuralism (seeking to decentre 'grand narrative' rationalism) or post-humanism (seeking to decentre the human from knowledge creation). However, despite the widespread appeal of these contemporary movements, a simple denial of humanism may allay the Cartesian dualism but in so doing initiates a new dualism of the post-human verses the human and so is powerless to stop perpetuating the interpretation of the world as human (or teleological). This can be demonstrated by an extreme reading of cosmism (Garis, 2005); where humanity is encouraged to not fear abandoning the human altogether and become entirely machine or AI. In such a scenario, we can question where these machines without need or want for anything would look for need or purpose but back towards their creators (as argued by Jorion, 2016). Therefore, any which way humanity or the human mind is conceptualises itself some form of subjective categorisation becomes undeniable.

This has meant that any contemporary accounts wishing to deny Cartesianism or humanism must nuance their perspective so as to acknowledge that any thought reliant on the subject destines any resulting philosophy to represent a correlation between the thinker and the world. For example, the trend of speculative realism is very cautious about asserting knowledge of the subject, instead, speculative realism tries to achieve an absolute in 'reality' free of the thinker, at the expense of demonstrating the subject's inability to ever represent reality entirely. Or other such nuanced approaches can be seen in the various theories of individuation or process (in the style of Simondon), whereby distinguishing subjects are never fully distinct and always in process or formation (see Garcia, 2014 for an account that seems to tread the line between both concerns). The process that speculative realism or individuation requires to distinguish their respective positions however, for example avoiding correlationalism, or asserting never-ending individuation or process still relies (as any argument does) on contrast (as implicitly real, or given) to make any of the concepts distinct from the other. Rather than 'radicalise the correlate' (i.e. to seek truth in the infinity implied in contradiction) to obscure the subject, or to enforce the process of individuation above and beyond the value of individual meanings, the approach I am advocating seeks new meanings from the contrast between opposing meanings and so sees no need to conflate subject with object, or thinker and the world, juxtaposing these positions, in contrast, means that they can be considered beyond an either-or relationship between the two.

Contrast makes it possible to make meaningful a cosmos both with and without the thinker, never knowing exactly what the subject or object is beyond the pre-requisite of contrast. To make meaning requires the subject to be juxtaposed in a simultaneously elevating as well as humbling position (Negarestani, 2018 is organised around a similar observation). The concept of the human is both the hero and casualty of the process of human thought. Humanity so happens to be the particular narrative that has been constructed around the circumstances inherited to us, but at the same time, the thinker can never escape the virtue of being something entirely apart from this narrative and one with the narrative of the rest of the universe. The point where that thought becomes the position of the universe and not exclusively the thinkers is impossible to say. In fact, it is the place of no one person or thing (or any absolute form) to say once and for all where subjects begin and end, rather all subjects and what they define themselves against (and all of their positionalities and philosophies) must exist all at once at the same time. Therefore, thought can never get beyond its own subject-hood (or object-hood), but as subjectivity grows so too does the appreciation of what it means to be in this position and so human. Even in extreme hypothetical examples such as in encounters with A.I. or other intelligent alien species, or if the subject were to find themselves struck with the revelation of being in a simulation (as proposed by Bostrom, 2003), the subject's understanding of itself is not erased but grows with the awareness of their situation. In this sense, the concept of the human or humanity may change, but a new word must necessarily come to replace it to refer to the collective subjectivity of likeminded beings. As a result, to advocate for a 'post' humanity seems to directly exacerbate the concerns of post-structuralism that prefigures it: i.e. 'the waning of affect' or the inability of the subject to assert their own authenticity (Jameson, 1991).

To argue for humanity in this way brings the argument back into contact with the legacy of Hegel's absolute idealism (Hegel's use of concepts such as spirit and humanity are reminiscent of the results of the table above, especially the way that these concepts share a complementary relationship across the wheel). In the Science of Logic, Hegel's own adage of Carteasianism decrees that "there is thinking, therefore there is something", is even more loaded than Descartes. Hegel's (1976) prophetic vision of unity leading to the assertion of history as a dialectic where humanity would become more and more conscious of its own spirit until absolutely aware of itself, taps into the heart of western ideology. This version of idealism radicalises the subject and its use of dialectic to the extent that knowledge of objects are unnecessary as they become dependent on the mind. This vision may seem extreme but its influence is so pervasive it is hard to suppress without it creeping in as an undercurrent. For example, even in post-structuralism's or post humanism's denial of grand narrative or humanism the question of spirit and teleology is still implicitly central even if subverted (see Braidotti, 2013). Ironically, it is Hegel's legacy which has served as a spectre over the human sciences since inception. The humanism presented in absolute idealism has proved notoriously difficult to escape from, as even the most ardent denial of humanism only serves to bolster its notoriety. Any criticism posed is always subjected to the subject (and therefore also human).[8] Humanism (in various guises) is present on both sides of the dominant political discourses of the 19th, 20th and 21st centuries, and despite the major reservations of post-structuralism (and now post-humanism) has remained intact even through the repeated inversions of opposing factions.

This reveals the productivity of the contradiction that humanity poses: of being universal whilst also only ever specific to the thinker. From this contradiction stems all of the controversies and elusiveness of the human mind, human soul and human spirit. The exact attributes of humanity may not be immediately identifiable, or directly quantifiable but are somehow also undeniable to the bearer. This is not to excuse the ambiguous role that evocations of the human spirit have had in the large-scale atrocities of the 20th century (for example, being difficult to untangle from both communism and national socialism). The method presented is bound to avow Hegel's legacy as much as it attempts to avert it.[9] For this reason, all undertones of teleology and absolutism need to be taken out of Hegel's interpretation of dialectic in order to find its continuing accuracy and pervasiveness. With the aid of the table above, it demonstrates the persistence of the human spirit as intractable from the concept of mind. To uphold one means to necessitate the other. For example, to deemphasise the human spirit (in favour of mind) accelerates capitalism's and modern science's tendency to de-authenticate the subject (or wane affect), whilst to emphasis the spirit (over mind) accelerates capitalism's counter tendency to radicalise the subject.[10] Through the questions posed by dualism as to what is human and what is not human, the result is that the intermediary of the spirit as both human and not becomes politicised (Jameson, 2014). However, unlike Hegel, spirit doesn't specifically need to be attached to the human or the subject, only anything that has contrast (contrast could be considered as much absolute idealism as it could be absolute empiricism). This process is at the heart of subjective experience and comes about each time the subject views an object; at the interface between the subject's perception of an object and the object's independent existence lies its spirit.[11] In this way, the spirit is at all times contrasted as it is both related to the subject and apart from the subject at the same time.[12] As a result, this simultaneously implies and denies both innatism and nativism as our thoughts are never our own and never fully part of the universe. Without spirt as an interface, there is no reason, meaning, thought, will or purpose to any of the other facets of humanity.

Therefore, it follows why these concepts have had such significance to western metaphysics. The question for these traditions has become avoiding any one philosophy from becoming absolute and therefore totalitarian, and is a task for which the method postulated and this book is engaged in. Just as metaphysics has sought to locate and accommodate humanity, metaphysics has needed to do so with a range of intermediary concepts between humanity and the universe humanity inhabits (as can be seen in the table above). The ultimate expression of this can be exampled through god; the god implied above symbolises the force that has provided for and continues to accommodate subjectivity and humanity. This is reminiscent of the argument from first cause which argues that because there can be seen to be a cause to things there must be a first cause, which can be equated to god (this argument is truly ancient and present in Aristotle, 1998 and beyond in pre-Socratic philosophy). This vision of god is not necessarily absolute, all-powerful and omnipotent, god is chiefly the being that enables humanity to exist, whether by random occurrence or divine patterning (which is also reminiscent of the philosophy of organism, or pragmatism). Conversely, this would make the devil a force that conspires to do the opposite opposing all subjectivity, reason and cause (being the exception to every rule). However, once the two are placed together (as in the table above) an even more supreme force can be glimpsed, one with more than one visage, one which can be said to be both reasonable and not at the same time, both subjective and beyond the subject, humane and inhumane (reminiscent of but surpassing Janus). The closest any concept comes to such a force is through contrast (as defined above). Contrast is both conceivable and inconceivable, omnipotent and yet impotent, absolute and infinite yet not all at the same time. To investigate humanities place in the universe inevitably produces some figure which relates the universe back to the human, but this figure is fated to contain many connotations each with some truth but also some fallacy (e.g. linking god to nothing, god to everything, god to creation, or god to absolution, god to possibility). In order for the subject to have any reflexive understanding of the world in which it has been placed it must do so with the ability to adapt reflection to differing eventualities whilst still reflecting back to the subject, as a result, the meaning of both god and the human (as well as all concepts) must revolve around something which is allows for infinite contrast. God challenges all those who seek to claim an absolute. E.g. for Melliassoux seeking an absolute contingency where anything is possible, god lies in the necessity of finitude and impossibility; for Derrida who seeks god in the desertification of language, god escapes in the miracle of god as an expression, and the list could go on inexhaustively. Therefore, the emphasis on contrast ensures that concepts do not become radicalised, made absolute or totalitarian. Even traditional absolute concepts such as god become subsumable by contrast. Contrast itself serves as the only absolute that is non-absolute, merely producing more contrast.

## Human

The position of taking the absolute as being non-absolute leaves some ambiguity as to the position of the thinker, as the argument above treats life, the human and the subject as almost (but not quite) interchangeable, what does this mean for the concept of the human of which we are bound? The adaptability of thought verses the always positioned subject gives a profound insight into the human condition. For one characteristic feature of the experience of being human is the ability to reflect, and this ability to reflect allows thought to take on more than one position; to imagine being in different positions or existing differently. However, when this ability to reflect is inevitably coupled with the unyielding position of always being situated as human it could also be seen to become a site of anguish around purpose and meaning (as in Kierkegaard, 2013 and; Sartre, 1992). Giving rise to existential questions of who we are, where we came from and where we are going. This dual characteristic of reflecting whilst situated is essential, as without it, there would be no experience of existence as there would be no distinction between thought and whatever opposes it. This could be used to imply the primacy of will and teleology as in the German idealism of Fichte (2000), or Schopenhauer's (1969) will to life or Nietzsche's (2017) will to power. However, rather than succumb to the same totalising, anthrocentric dangers of these accounts, this characteristic of reflection whilst situated also implies that the acquisition of knowledge and experience relies upon the death of old knowledge and experience in some way. This describes a perilous and contradictory position for thought as on the one hand, constantly transforming whilst on the other having nowhere concrete to place the self. The experience of the self is the experience of being opposed and so the self cannot be stored outside contrast. As a result, will is always in the shadow of contrast. This contradiction marks the profundity of the concept of what it is to be human, which is both internal and external to the self.

As has been argued in the section above, the human can be wholly removed from humanity whilst the subjectivity it implies cannot. This makes the distinction between the human and the subject small, but none the less significant. As a result, the human has many different contrasts, because our existence does not just accord to one concept alone. The human could conform to anything that contrasts human existence e.g. the animal, or monster, but the most overarching concept (and perhaps most problematic) used to describe this opposition to the human would be that of nature (and so here the meaning of the human is very close to that of culture). Therefore, the concept of nature is particular to the cosmos that a specific human uses to relate with the world. As anthropological sources such as Descola (2013) attest, some human groups without experience of modernity (such as Amazonian tribes) do not necessarily split nature and culture. In this sense, nature must also hold many meanings, and potentially different dialectics. To some extent, this explains the fascination and mystery behind making and comparing translations between languages. Relating to another being relies on an understanding of what that being takes as anterior to themselves, if the sense of anteriority is lost so too is their distinction as a being and the impetus for relation. This means that nature cannot be seen as contrast or contradiction alone (as is much contended in idealism see Breazeale, 2014). Nature is as much defined by contrast as the human is, meaning that the concepts share a complex and contingent relationship that is not only contradictory. To position nature in this way stands the questions of humanism (and existentialism) on its head as instead of looking for authenticity inwards toward the human or outwards to nature (i.e. as lead by Cartesian first principles) the question of authenticity is opened out into the contrast between, outside of both reason, the subject and what they oppose. This enquiry is as much contemporary (i.e. in post-humanism), as it is ancient. It is for this reason that Confucius can be quoted as saying that: "The understanding that arises from authenticity is called our nature" and a meaningful translation can be posed to echo through the ages, never quite capturing the meaning entirely but never lost whilst there is still an unbroken link to history of the languages.[13] Charting the concept of human and nature as they appear in English makes distinct Western philosophies entanglement in a much larger human narrative:

**Figure IV-3**

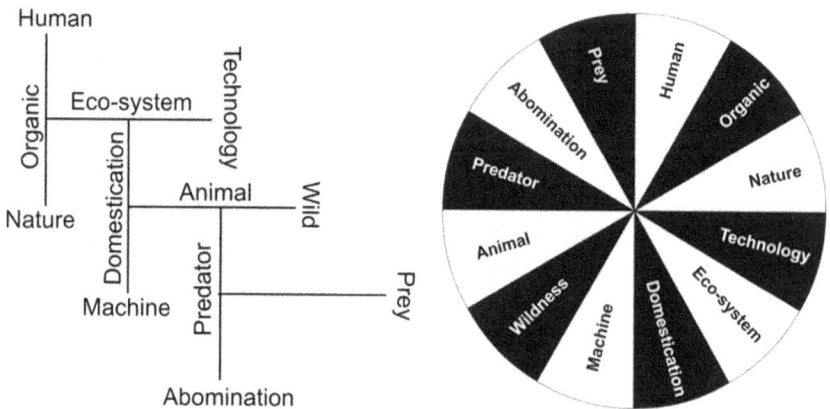

**Table IV-3**

| Human | Oikos/ecosystem (nurture) | Animal |
|---|---|---|
| The human is a highly contested concept. At its most undeniable it is anyone directly relatable and to ourselves as kin. Consequently, evil thrives from both the denial of and the embrace of humanity. | Between the organic and non-organic is the oikos, a system of constituent parts working together towards distinct and individual purposes. | Between the wild and domesticated is the animal. That which shares a similar condition as ourselves but also has its own sense of nature and is therefore also wild. |
| Nature | Machine | Abomination |
| The human has more than one possible opposite, but | Opposing an eco-system a machine is a series of part working together to fulfil a | The opposite of an animal is that which is contrary to human intervention and has |

| | | |
|---|---|---|
| only one ultimate one, which is everything that is not human. The most ultimate version of this is nature. The difficulty of this concept lies in its highly relative nature, e.g. a human must contradictorily be both a part of this nature whilst also apart.<br><br>Organic<br><br>Between a human and nature is the concept of all things that can be said to be alive in a similar and relative way to the human; i.e. organic.<br><br>Technology<br><br>The opposite of organic is the non-organic. This can be argued to be technology, which will be taken to mean here as that which is wilfully created. | definite and particular and purpose.<br><br>Domestication<br><br>Between technology and oikos is the concept of domestication. This is the creation of a system in accordance with but independent of human intervention. The concept of cultivation could also be considered here.<br><br>Wildness<br><br>The opposite of domestication is that which lives in discord to the sphere of human intervention and is inaccessible to cultivation (the contradiction here is that the characteristic of something will always be wild, even when domesticated it is the characteristic element which remains much like the spirit). | an inverse sense of nature, which would be termed as a monster or abomination.<br><br>Predator<br><br>Between an animal and an abomination is a predator which is that which preys on others to achieve its domestication.<br><br>Prey<br><br>The opposite of a predator is a prey: that which is consumed in the process of another's domestication. Therefore, the human is between predator and prey, being both whilst also neither. The reflexive human finds itself in a keystone position to nature, choosing to be either predator or prey as part of their nature. |

The results of the table above continue the Western anthopocentric theme of highlighting 'the world according to us' as opposed to 'the world against us'. If the human and nature are opposed, neither may exclusively be said to possess or be the origin of the contrast of which has been argued throughout this book.[14] Contrast must be a unifying force which initiates but is also simultaneously separate from both the human and nature. Chiefly, this is represented in the form of a line in which the motivations for human activity (according to Western modernity) are engaged. The contrast between wildness and cultivation is extremely fine. This leads to a number of significant contradictions as if the human is cultivated then it must be at the expense of nature where only the human is allowed to run wild or vice versa; if nature is cultivated then it must be at the expense of the human where only nature is allowed to run wild. This line could be questioned as arbitrary but to do so is to negate its necessity to produce meaning to the narrative of the human. As a result, distinguishing between the line between what is human and what is nature is highly idiosyncratic and ephemeral, but also very heavily defended as can most boldly be seen written into the various conventions of human rights and constitutional charters proclaiming freedom and equality. To give the human narrative meaning the line must be rehearsed over and again in order to instate and maintain what is valuable for the human and the world that humans inhabit (very obvious treading of these lines can be seen throughout Romanticism, Gothicism and Environmentalism). This is because as a human, the process of domestication dictates moral and ethical direction of how we should live our lives both separately and apart.

The root of this experience belongs to the subject specified as human, and the contradiction that entails. This contradiction is immortalised as 'the human condition' and conveniently aggregated to the search for the purpose and meaning of life. Beyond this human search for purpose and meaning, however, other existences ulterior to the human is also undeniable and continues whether individuals search for it or not. For this reason, the contrast against the subjective could be considered as the mother of all narratives (and Collingwood, 1960 provides a good account for how narratives of nature have developed). Combinations of concepts in Western literature that tread the line of the human v nature, or nature v human, or nature working with the human, or the human without nature are ceaselessly abundant. In turn, these narratives grant authenticity to subjective accounts and in so doing belief, purpose and meaning. As a result, such accounts are unavoidable and intractable from experience. It goes to the very heart of the contrast between the human and nature. The Western concept of the human is wholly reliant in this sense on nature, both the human and nature must both be authentic, or both be a construction. The human is neither the Ptolemaic centre nor the Copernican periphery of the cosmos, nature or existence, each one runs through the human in every direction and dimension. Nature is the great beyond to human meaning. This results in a major contradiction as both the human and nature must exist as supreme but yet tolerate the supremacy of the other. The further that nature is described as illusory, the more everything becomes nature. The more that everything is described as nature, the less there can be any. Any claim to post-humanity or post-nature – explored in work such as Latour (1993), Haraway (1991) or Morin (1979), and as they themselves uphold – results in partiality because opposing categories of the human and nature are needed to make any sense of the other, ourselves or our position in the universe. To surpass them would rely upon an entirely different cosmos and order to Western modernist thinking. Any such surface attempt may adapt the terminology, and even their meanings, but something akin to the contrast of human and nature remains undeniable as long as thought is positioned in any kind of body aspiring to rationality.

This can be used to assess the partiality of dominant narratives of the human in nature that the present epoch has inherited. The most fervent contemporary discussions of this dualism have been around evolutionary theory (a project which has produced many heroes and villains from Darwin and Cuvier to Lamarck). Evolutionism has spanned multiple disciplinary branches and inspired many interpretations including the legitimisation of many moral and political agendas. Two major discordant interpretations could be drawn from these discussions, most recognisable as nature v nurture. Interpretations of evolution as nature put a strong emphasis on the biological aspects of natural selection. They assume a dominance on the power of nature driving random mutations that make certain organisms more likely to survive in a certain environment. Whilst contrasting interpretations of this understanding of natural selection as nurture, conversely assert the ways in which the habits or choices of certain organisms may shape the future existence of their offspring and consequent species.[15] This ongoing contradiction spans many disciplines and defines how much choices are determined by external forces verses an individual's capacity to make choices (or personality). Explicit in scientific debate since at least the time of Tinbergen's (1951) 'study of instinct' which surmises that behaviour must be considered as both reactionary and spontaneous (or can be traced even further back to Yerkes and Dodson, 1908). But despite the frankness of the debate, such an emphasis has made it hard to assimilate the human and the processes of evolution (see Fuentes, 2017). The opposing narratives of the human in control of their destiny, whilst all the time simply a slave to evolution have led to extremely opposing philosophical conclusions. For example, it can be used as a justification for nihilistic ideas of humans evolving with no meaning or purpose as much as it can be highjacked into discourses such as German idealism's understanding of will (and contradiction) as a natural force to assert dangerous notions that evolution is a progress to ever more greatness and sophistication. Therefore, alluding evolution to dialectic alone is problematic.

Idealisms portrayal of ecology prioritises human choice as somehow separate and above the choices of other family species, confusing the status of choice in shaping what is construed as nature. For example, the inherited wisdom of idealism such as Hegel (2004) or Bataille (1990) deny the animal reflexivity and so fail to account for the destiny or purpose of an animal as aside from that of nature in general. Although not exclusive to idealism this view came to dominate the humanism of the 19th and 20th centuries. Running parallel to these narratives has been the concept of umwelt which emphasises that each organism perceives its own environment differently (Von Uexkull, 2009). This initiated a question about how to account for perspective and truth that consumed 20th-century philosophy. On the one hand, it could be argued that there is no one truth, only perspective (as in existentialism or process philosophies), and on the other that perspective is meaningless and should be detached from truth as much as possible (as in empiricism). The outcome of these debates on both sides served only to obscure environment, as either position emphasises a human's place in the world, and not on a universe beyond the human. To counter, contemporary narratives have sought to incorporate (whilst surpassing) both by placing an increasing emphasis on philosophical and political narratives of the human and nature as interdependent where family trees (and keystone species) must rely on and exist together borderlessly for each other's benefit (see Timofeeva, 2018). Or at the other extreme, speculative realism could be read as demonstrating nature's total indifference to the human. Therefore, to distinguish contrast from a view of will as hierarchical or the other extreme of abandoning will entirely, requires both the distinctions and similarities between the human, animal and nature to be accommodated as one in the same thing. Contrast alone cannot shape matter, and matter without contrast does not matter (i.e. hold any significance), this must mean our evolution fits into a much more profound narrative of which the human is a part of as well as separated from. This has been broached in biology as teleonomy (coined by Pittendrigh, 1958 to distinguish it from the theological concept of teleology; also see Mayr, 1961). All organisms that have branched into two families believe in different things and at some point, relatives of one branch have made an opposite choice to branch off in the name of survival. The opposing choices of one species ensure the survival of the other, most obviously seen in predators and prey/carnivore and herbivore. The ways in which organisms live and believe in what they sense influences the growth and decline of their body and the results of these changes alter their epigenetics, and their choice of habitat and who they choose to exist and mate with. Acts such as diet; cannibalism; rearing offspring; and mating all imply a belief and ongoing choices. The difficulty of including belief, choice, will, habit and personality into interpretations of natural selection may have partially obscured what exactly evolution has come to mean. For example, such controversy implies an emphasis on natural selection as deterministic. Through such a skew evolution emphasises the need for survival over and above the need to thrive. Without the sense of thriving, there is no point or meaning to survival. Belief and choice form the basis of a life spent not merely surviving but thriving and in so doing making survival meaningful, and therefore to all organisms, choice is essential as their inheritance and the surroundings of which they find themselves (for which the pioneering ecologist Ricketts, 2006 offers a novel account of viewing this deeper meaning). Conversely to explain choice using a force such as that of idealisms 'will', links the human will to that found in all life but distorts the human's position to nature through the human's extra access to reflexivity. Telos or purpose cannot be found in subjects or objects, but only in their ratio. This highlights that either referring to all creation as natural, or conversely all creation as idealistic (or nurture) alone represents an extreme and partial perspective. In order to maintain the order between the two, the concept of contrast must be used as an independent force that simultaneously belongs to both and neither. To ensure that neither definition becomes dominant, the process of evolving should be seen as much as a kind of symbioticism as it is a determinism. Consider how the evolution of life evolve does not ripple to in regiment to ever grander or smaller scales as does energy, predators do not grow ever larger and consummate unto entropy, rather the intelligence of life evolves not to exhaust its medium. This could even be taken further to question at which point the evolution of life can be determined from the continual flux of the inorganic matter around it.

The points raised here are by no means new, but taken together they allude to the necessity of the contrast between life and nature to the process of creating will, meaning, reason or purpose. Contrast is not reducible to nature any more than the reflexive thoughts or ideals that conceive it, rather it is in the active juxtaposition between all things which inadvertently generates all their other meanings and purpose. Will, choice and purpose are not prescriptive, shallow or superficial, rather through contrast (and its indefinability) they are imprinted onto the infinite. This is significant because firstly it implies that the human is the result of not only human belief and choices, but those of many other organisms, and secondly that through belief and choice we are connected to the actions and reactions of the wider universe, we never become more or less that any of the forces which oppose us (notwithstanding the timeliness of the question in terms of climate crisis Mickey, 2016; Morton, 2016). Therefore, the line between the human and nature holds a productive contradiction intractable from meaning, belief or purpose, rather than being a reductive to an either/or division.

## The Individual

The debates around the meaning of the human v nature uncovered here have a wide relevance to the human sciences. The human/nature divide is associated with one of the most contested questions in the discipline; of whether to consider society as having a meaningful existence beyond the individuals who constitute it. Such distinctions were present right from the inception of sociology; for Durkheim (2014) external social realities exist in the outer world and are independent of the individual's perception of them, whilst for Weber (1949) society was only ever to be found through interpretation. Following these early discussions, the development of the discipline has flourished into ever more intricate nuances, all such concerns however, tread a very similar line to that demarcated between the human and nature. Coincidentally, the development of the social sciences has been parallel with that of evolution and as a result, the same discussions around evolution have become intertwined in debates about society. Multifarious dispositions exist in the human sciences with varying acceptances or disavowals of evolution. Accounts range from using evolution as a means to understand society (e.g. in the social Darwinism of Herbert Spenser now debunked, or in modern tenants of naturalism), to viewing evolution as a means to differentiate human society against that which it originates and often opposes. The pitfalls and dangers of these positions have been well documented and 20C[th] history is littered with the scars caused (encapsulated in the controversies still surrounding Darwin, 1871). Far from being conclusive, evolution still holds a partial shell to society that is tricky to escape from, sometimes this shell is recognisable on the forms and functions of society (e.g. consider how the free market is conceptualised and justified, or how history is still defined in terms of the cultural evolutionary terms of Jurgenson Thomsen, i.e. the Stone, Bronze and Iron ages) but is never adequate to fully capture its intricacy. Once initiated, these discussions have been fuelled by the belief that the enrichment of life lies in the endeavour that all things human (and relating to the human) should become knowable. The danger of this endeavour has been that regardless of whether sociological accounts confirm or refute evolution, the question of 'what a human should resemble' or 'how human life should be conducted' are forwarded by both sides of the debate. Foucault (2001b, pp. 523–4) demonstrates this concern, when arguing for his work to be used as a toolkit rather than reach conclusions that may justify actions that would feed into the same endeavour he sought to expose. To take this contestation further, any one concept taken on mass to an extreme or as an absolute (e.g. to assert that society is 'evolutionary') results in more partial social realities that can have certain benefits or drawbacks for the individual. For example, in liberal democracy, this is most often polemicized in the differences between Rousseau and Hobbes on whether human nature is inherently good or bad. This translates into whether governance should be legitimated towards the individual or the collective; vis-à-vis the goal of society is to allow the individual to thrive, verses the goal of society should be to thrive collectively. At their heart, the necessity of one informs the necessity of the other, and so the further any extreme is pushed the more partiality is emphasised. This process is to some extent unavoidable for it is impossible to avoid taking a position.

In history understood as either dialectical or rhetorical between the individual and society, the oppositions held by individuals or between whole societies are the quintessence of society. This implies that society is symmetrical in the same ways in that concepts are (especially pertinent seen as it is from concepts that social realities arise). Even if in many cases the exactness of that symmetry is hard to distinguish without retrospect. From such a perspective, the polarities of left and right that have dominated political thought are to be expected (or could be exampled with the Dionysian v Apollonian invoked by Nietzsche, 2008 among others). At their extremes, both ideologies of the left, of extreme collectivism, or of the right, of extreme individualism have been shown to hold dangers, i.e. holding the state above the individual or holding the individual above the state. Resistance is therefore located in the quality of the narrative, and in the avoidance of extremes (as demonstrated by Popper, 2012). However, even this stance has its pitfalls as can be seen in the radical centrism of late 20thC third way politics. The express agenda to avoid extremes can be viewed ironically as an extreme initiating the political apathy which has contributed to modern societies being susceptible to more emotive extremes (such as the fanatic agendas forwarded by fake news and privacy issues in recent social media scandals Han, 2018). It seems that no discourse is spared this fate, as just as with Hegel before him, even the legacy of Foucault who tirelessly disavowed any one particular political position, has become entangled with the same controversies as with the neoliberal centrisms that have arisen since his death (Lagasnerie, 2012; Zamora and Behrent, 2015).[16] These examples force us to accept that no one answer alone is responsible, and accept that the very concept of utopian rule is an extreme that is also regrettably unavoidable to ponder. Beneath every civilisation is a question of the value of individual life (or the most generic form of subjectivity) v the value of collective will (the most generic form of objectivity). To make the world in our image or to let it be itself. The names, connotations and exactitudes of the concepts may differ, but once one is implied so is the other. In this way, contrast is comparable to all concepts whilst not reducible to, and out of reach of any one specific definition. For this reason, the distinction can be traced through all justifications denoting 'barbarians' from 'civilised peoples'.[17] Any denigration of one civilisation's value of individual life onto another civilisation demonstrates an equal and opposite reflection of the values of life over collective will.[18]

Idealism, evolution or any such singular explanation fails because the functions of society does not occur as the result of one order or even one set of orders, but through contrast which is always by definition evasive of any one singular mode of interpretation. To see the effect of contrast on the concept of society, the dialectic/rhetoric method can once again be deployed:

**Figure IV-4**

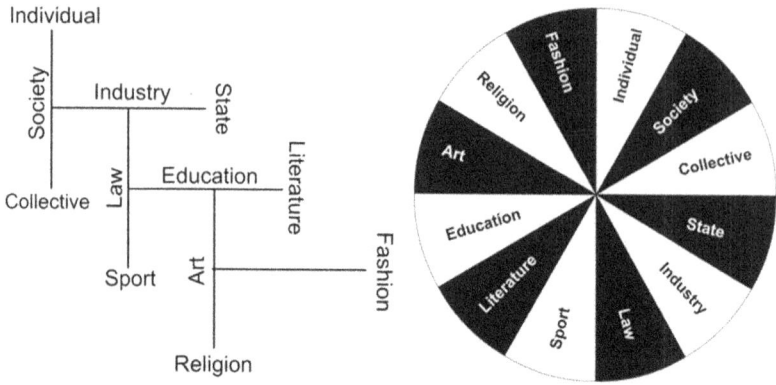

**Table IV-4**

| Individual | Industry | Education |
|---|---|---|
| The individual is one person's will on their own. | Between the society and state is industry which is the productivity of the individual, and collective managed closely by the state. In this case, industry is bound up administratively and with business and commerce. | Between law and literature, education seeks to inform individuals, society and cultures on the replication of its legal and literal values. |
| Collective | | Religion |
| Opposite to the individual is the collective will of a group of individuals. | | The opposite of education is religion which indoctrinates rather than informs value unto individuals, societies and cultures through the upholding of ritual and tradition. The line between religion and education may be fine, as each relies upon the other to ensure that one separates from the other. |
| Society | Sport | |
| Between the individual and the collective is society, a collective of individuals grouping themselves together.[19] (Margaret Thatcher famously declared that there is no society only individuals, seen here society is as undeniable as the individual, and the statement can be demonstrated as rhetorical). | The opposite to industry is sport, which is individual, societal and cultural activity for recreation and not production. | |
| | Law | Art |
| | Between industry and sport is law: the rules abided by individuals, societies and cultures to dictate the line between production and recreation. | Between education and religion art seeks to uncover the sacred and the reverent. Art teaches as much as it ensues reverence. |
| State | Literature | Fashion |
| The opposite of the society is the state, which is the entity employed to regulate society. | The opposite of law is literature, literature inspires rather than dictates how | The opposite of art is fashion which seeks to define the most acceptable mode of practice for |

| | individuals should enact and think about the line between production and recreation rather that dictates it. (Includes narratives, dramatisation etc.). | the moment at hand (nowness), not scared to render things un-sacred or to break established rules in the name of what is called for at a particular moment. Between art and fashion, fashion and society the individual finds a mode within which to consolidate themselves with all other activities.[20] |
|---|---|---|

The resulting series of categories is reminiscent of 'pillars of a civilisation' like Plato's (1987a) republic. Such an interpretation however, should only proceed with extreme caution. Notable attempts of the past to uncover universal human categories such as Jung's archetypes or Levi-Strauss's structuralism have been largely ignored or eventually disbanded in social theory. Any attempt to chart the essential faculties of a society inadvertently become a standard from which to judge the quality of individual lives, thereby intensifying the pressure on individuals to conform to societal standards. For example, over time, the standards of Plato's republic or Confucius are inevitably contentious to extended generations or societies. However, to not enshrine some faculties as essential is to place the ideals of a society totally outside the reach of individuals and lose the benefits of social engagement. Therefore, the entanglement between ideas of societal structure with idealised value judgments are to some extent unavoidable. To deny such an entanglement is to disband the meaning of distinctions entirely. Such interpretations are perpetuated by individuals, but beyond the control of any one individual. Therefore, simultaneously these categories can be interpreted as providing aspirational motives for those who subscribe to any one of the concepts – whilst at the same time as a means of coercing non-subscribers to fit into societal norms they may have no will to be a member of. A view of contrast in these categories makes it possible to consider their unrestricted value at the same time as their limit. The constitution of the categories does not reside in the individual or the collective, but rather in the contrast between the two.

Any one of the concepts forms an interdependent schema that is totally reliant on the other concepts to provide its meaning. As a result, in themselves, these concepts do not constitute an absolute form, but each relies on the contradictions and contraventions of the other to inspire activity and breathe life into them. Through their combined existence each category offers the possibility to be imprisoned by or escape from the last. Individuals can either choose to engage in them or face being enrolled by them, as non-compliance still constitutes engagement. Therefore, these categories are idealised modes of engagement, whilst at the same time being beyond any one individual. Together these activities perform a regulatory function for the society and the individual at the same time as providing a site of resistance (this is significant as using the method postulated demonstrates this engagement to incorporate both of the hitherto contradictory positions of Foucault's 1977; interpersonal disciplinary actions and Althusser's 2005 top-down ideological state apparatus). Combined with narratives of nature v culture, these categories provide meaning and purpose to the individuals, societies and environments that support them. Once formed these activities develop institutions around the extreme concept positions made necessary by the concept of the individual v. the collective. Each of these extremes then becomes idealised and re-established by individuals who commit to a particular narrative of civilization. It is therefore impossible to denote with exact precision where these categories begin or end. In the everyday course of human activities, many different infractions and affirmations react to and resist these categories and result in the blurring of the lines between where one category begins, and one ends. However, as an aggregate beyond any one individual the totality of the distinctions becomes tangible and makes engagement or resistance possible.

The concepts uncovered cannot be said to be either fully universal or particular to individuals or individual cultures. The precise manner in which these concept form in any particular society remains highly specific. Essentially the chart above places the definition for society in contrast to the individual. As such, these dynamics are therefore neither fully ideals, nor only to be found reflecting wider forces beyond the individual, rather they rely on the simultaneous interaction between both ideals and their opposition. This perspective modifies the overwhelming preoccupations of social theory from previous generations, caught in debating to various degrees the extent to which the constituents of society can be seen to be 'constructed' or only ever as ideal (e.g. rationalism, social constructionism, post structuralism) vs. various forms of realisms or materialisms (e.g. the varying incarnations of positivism, historical materialism, STS or ANT). Through using the method postulated, contrast can be seen to be common to and productive of all of the contested distinctions of these past debates. In this respect, society maintains the same contradiction as nature; simultaneously belonging to but also always beyond the individual, as all concepts are subject to a larger force of contrast.

This highlights the ongoing anxiety of the human sciences on asserting the authenticity, translatability and replication of concepts. If the effect of contrast and connotation at work between all concepts is infinite this can be interpreted to mean that either concepts are in constant transformation but bound to contrast or are static but never-ending. As a result, observations between different individuals, societies and cultures struggle for absolute accuracy because of the potential for individual discrepancy. This clashes with the predominate concerns of the social sciences and humanities in the 19th and 20th century to compare and contrast between categories or institutions free from any one particular perspective or lens (e.g. the so-called sociological imagination). Such concerns were judged to have a preoccupation with authenticity, which led the social sciences of the late 20th and early 21st century to look beyond questions of authentication (such as Actor Network Theory, process philosophy or speculative materialism). But what such movement discovered were that they must either tread the line between tolerating contrary perspectives as equally valid at the expense of the authenticity of their own account (such as process philosophy); or disavow contrary perspectives as valid but risk their account becoming dogmatic and so also threaten the authenticity of their own account.[21] In both of these approaches, the only authenticity certain is that of their inevitable contradiction. Therefore, only the contrast as sensed allows concepts to be both authentic and particular. If contrast is accepted as being as intrinsic to the patterns found in nature as it is to the thoughts of an individual, the objects that concepts refer to are embraced in the same relationship as ideals. Objects are distinct from the concepts used to describe them but also exist independently of the individual in the same patterns that thoughts are made from (my attempt here is to contradict as much as confirm materialism with idealism). As a result, the authentication of social realities is to be found in their contrasts. The more a concept is taken away from that which it contrasts the more it transforms into something else. As a result, concepts such as the individual or society are very hard to consider on their own.

## Rules and Exceptions

Beyond the particularities of individuals or their social realities, the dynamics of the meanings uncovered seem to reflect the dynamics of all the concepts covered in this book. In the tables above the similarity between concepts and the thing they represent emerges through their ratio to each other. In most of the history of ideas, contrast has played a hidden role in the background of discourse. The method used here inverts this pursuit and attempts to make possible a view of meaning as non-neutral (i.e. a view of meanings as meaningful even when opposed). Rather than result in chaos or meaninglessness some rules have emerged. Principally, a rule for contrast; that for any rule there is always an exception (or to paraphrase Cicero, that the exception proves the rule). This may be hard to fully accept as it is counterintuitive. To accept any singular concept as authentic, requires that concept to be opposed to the contrast from which it emanates. Conflictingly, this renders concepts as in contact with both authenticity and inauthenticity.

Untangling the relationship between the two cannot be done by focusing on singular concepts alone, rather the meaning of a concept is part of an interdependent spectrum which relies on ratio and opposition for distinction and form. This characteristic means that each concept is as distinct as it is dynamic. Concepts are neither fully idealistic nor merely correlated between different versions of reality, rather concepts emerge from the contrast between the transcendence of thought (and rationality) and the physicality of being situated (and emotional). Between the two, contrast is contrasted infinitely. Thought is part of this process that is at the same time universal and particular. Therefore, conceiving meaning relies on an approach that's both deductive and inductive where both dialectic and rhetoric are considered.

Dialectic is a means to authenticate concepts beyond any one individual perspective. In the process, dialectic allows thought to transcend being situated in one individual, but in so doing has the tendency to become desynchronised from actuality. Alternately, rhetoric de-authenticates concepts by demonstrating that every rule has an exception. This is as a means to synchronise ideas back to the individuals they are situated within. Rather than pit them against each other as has been done since the time of Plato and Aristotle (or Parmenides and Heraclitus) I wish to consider the ways in which they are entangled. Each one relies on the other as the authenticity of meaning is easily corrupted by argument. To adopt or dismiss any one side of an argument is done in the face of ignoring how each side of any argument is reliant upon the other. However, it is also impossible to consider any argument without taking a position (even if that position is indifference). Both rhetoric and dialectic are therefore needed to gain a perspective on the meaning of a concept free from argument and connotation; e.g. if one concept is taken as a rule then another one is needed in order to be its exception:

**Figure IV-5**

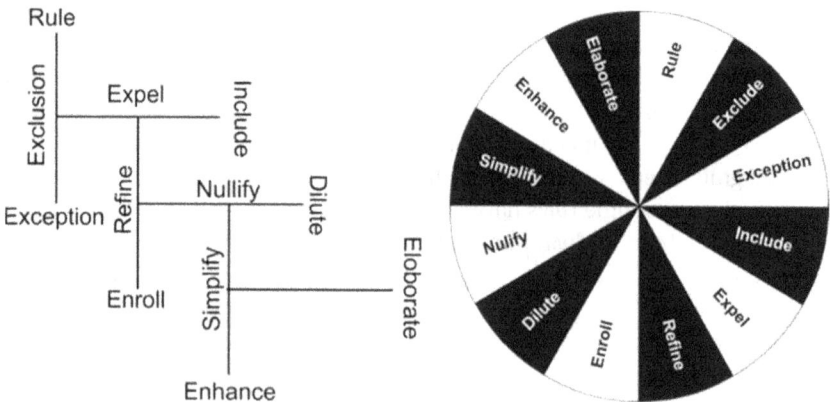

**Table IV-5**

| Rule (effect) | Expel | Nullify |
|---|---|---|
| A rule is a regulation or principle governing conduct or procedure within a particular system or area of activity. In this sense, a rule is also the existence of a system. | Between inclusion and exclusion; to expel or dismiss is to exclude something that is already included out of the system of rules. | Between refinement and dilution is nullification. To nullify is to render something as having no effect in a particular system of rules. |
| **Exception** | **Enrol** | **Enhance** |
| The opposite of a rule is its exception, which is the point where a rule no longer applies (I had grappled with the concept of anomie here, before concluding that the opposite of a rule is not the state of rulelessness, as such a state is still a rule, and so the opposite of a rule should be considered an exception that evades all rules). | The opposite of dismissing is to enrol; to not recognise something as being in the same system of rules as the one you are trying to create but to attempt to bring it into the system. | The opposite of nullifying is to enhance. Enhancement means that the power of something is increased in a certain system of rules. |
| | **Refine** | **Simplify** |
| **Exclusion** | Between dismissing and enrolment is to refine; to take some elements of something but to exclude others. | Between nullification and enhancement is simplification. To simplify is to both nullify non-effective aspects and enhance the most effective aspects of something until its position in a system of rules is more apparent and conflating elements have been removed. |
| Between a rule and its exception is an exclusion which is to place something apart altogether from a system decrying rules or exceptions. | **Dilute** | |
| | The opposite of refining is to dilute, which is to make something less potent through mixing it with something innocuous. (The diluting mixtures innocuousness must be related to the system of rules you are attempting to create, as through making something diluted it is being brought into a system of rules). | **Elaborate** |
| **Inclusion** | | The opposite of simplification is to elaborate. To elaborate is to continue to add more relevant elements to a system of rules. Something that is both simplified and elaborate forms the basis of a rule, as does something elaborated that excludes certain things from it. The middle point between both sets of concepts points to a process for creating rules. |
| The opposite of exclusion is inclusion; to incorporate wider factors into a system of rules. | | |

This table contains a method from which to approach concepts in accordance with the rhetoric/dialectic method already demonstrated. From the negation of the concept of a rule, a set of rules still emerge. However, these rules are a contradiction in terms; either the table could be taken to mean that all things (that are possible to observe as 'things') are part of one rule, or all things are an exception to. Therefore, all things must be both a rule and exception to a rule at the same time. This is a rather confusing outcome, but can be taken to mean that all things meaningful must form part of a self-contained system that defines their meaning and position to each other. The table above constitutes a means to accommodate observable things into a system of meaning. It demonstrates a set of principles that aim to simplify complex realities into workable systems. Such attempts are the mainstay of most secularised epistemological thinking (e.g. Aristotle's 1889 Organon, or Kant's 2007 categories of understanding). The classification system of the table above can be compared to the principle of falsification (as discussed earlier), in the sense that a concept can be authenticated against the concepts that they are opposed to. However, when compiled, rather than only going in the direction of falsification (i.e. that any rule has an exception), the method above goes in the opposite direction also; (that which is an exception has the potential to also become a rule). As a result, the resulting principle looks more heuristic like the less logically rigorous but more generalisable Occam's razor; the principle that the simplest solution is the most accurate (a principle that is found in a wide array of sources from Newton to Ptolemy). Here it could be taken to mean that when authenticating the meaning of a concept the one with the least connotations is the most authentic. The accuracy of the principle can be placed in the contrast between the individual attempting to work out singular experiences against a boundless and infinite surrounding universe. Placing concepts in contrast (i.e. in direct opposites) allows for a perspective on their meaning which requires the least amount of further inference possible, allowing for them to be re-conveyed more authentically. The more inference placed on a concept, the less likely it is to convey accurately the contrast from which its meaning is derived. This makes subjectivity the experience of setting a boundary against a vast and boundless infinite contrast. Accordingly, this would depict free thought as the ultimate tool allowing finite beings to be able to live as a situated part of an infinite universe that is both immensely bigger and smaller than it (in all dimensions simultaneously).

By accepting this contradiction (or accepting something beyond the logic of it), the acquisition of knowledge is less a question of absolution, or even degrees of certainty, but rather direction (reminiscent of the debates on demarcation between Popper, 1974; Kuhn, 1970; Lakatos, 1968; and Feyerabend, 1993). Any one concept taken too far becomes distorted. For example, concepts as applied to scientific method must be constantly tested, as once taken outside of the context from which they were isolated, controlled and tested will inevitably distort the further they are taken from the original context. This may seem reasonable as it underlies the scientific discourse upon which contemporary society is foundered, but once the contrasting nature of meaning is accounted for, the observation of diverse phenomena may not be added up into one whole or complete overview without an overlapping contrast. Even though modern science accounts for many uncertainties (e.g. the Copenhagen interpretation)[22] contemporary philosophy (including the philosophy of science) still holds, in varying degrees, an unease towards uncertainty in fear of incoherence and de-authentication. Realigning scientific discovery with philosophy will require the prevalent understandings of logic, rationality, emotion and authenticity (etc.) to accommodate contrast not only as a toleration, but as the foundation of their necessity. Concepts once considered 'poison' can become 'medicine'; 'improvements' can become 'impairments'; 'better' can become 'worse' and 'good' can become 'bad' and vice versa. The more any one concept is used and held in disregard of the opposition of others the more it becomes saturated and distorted. Regardless of the sensitivity or reflexivity of a concept's application, if taken to extremes against opposition, that concept's corruption is inevitable. Every concept therefore has the potential to become distorted, and any regime that is based around certain concepts when pushed into the extreme corners of whole societies has the ability to cause as many wrongs as rights.

This has obvious ethical ramifications. According to the table, ethics cannot be considered as either solely deontological (or idealistic or based on virtues of an idealistic rule) or ontological (or consequential, circumstantial, procedural or to render to this schema, based on exception), but rather both. This implies that no concept alone should be considered as either fully ethical or unethical. If ethics is unintelligible without establishing intent and consequence, either only becomes discernible in reciprocation, and nothing is more exemplary of this than the golden rule; 'do to others as you would have done to yourself', so-called because it is accounted for in nearly all cultures and religions (and contrasted against its opposite of duplicity). The golden rule exemplifies a meaning that is not unidirectional (i.e. it allows the direction of ethics to be changeable), and so represents a means to make contradictions operational. However, even this rule is not without controversy, for example, it doesn't take account for the threshold of what constitutes another individual and also ignores what may be necessary 'evils' (for example, most people but not all would agree that cannibalism violates the golden rule, fewer would agree that eating other animals does and fewer still would see a plant as an other on a par with themselves). Many notable philosophical examples (such as Kant, 2008; Nietzsche, 2009) demonstrate how the golden rule by itself is insufficient to produce a complete system of ethics. However, no such position either ideal or actual manages to be freed from it entirely as reciprocity is always present even if what that reciprocity means relies on processes of individuation that are not always fully apparent.

Ethics is necessary as a means to attune personal belief to wider, independent and dynamic realities. As such, they are both logical and anti-logical at the same time. Such beliefs are only meaningful if they have the chance to be proven untrue, as if they were already true, then they would be fact and not subject to ethics. Therefore, no such all-encompassing rule of ethics can exist as such a rule would render choice meaningless, contravening the need for ethics in the first place.

The challenge of maintaining such an understanding of ethics as inherently meaningful is to avoid the opposing extremes of moral relativism or nihilism. I.e. to say that meaning is not meaningful because it comes from and will go back to nothing, or that it is (e.g. 'life is an unprofitable episode disturbing the blessed calm of non-existence' Schopenhauer, 2007). To counter nihilism requires a principle with which to founder meaning. The response, according to the method postulated has been; that the only fact can be that there is no one incontrovertible fact alone. On the surface, this may seem to be relativistic, closer inspection however reveals a key difference. Even at the most extreme position of nihilism, something must be believed in or it would be impossible to articulate the position in the first place (turning the arguments of Brassier, 2007; or Land, 2018 on their heads). Moreover, relativism must also concede that a belief that nothing is absolute constitutes an absolute i.e. that of nothing. If existence is ultimately meaningless, this only demonstrates another contrast as meaninglessness requires the concept of meaning to become meaningful. This is proof that both relativism and nihilism must be part of some larger guiding pattern or meaning to make any relation meaningful at all. Without both relation and difference, there is no meaning. This means that even from the perspective of nihilism a belief in meaning is inevitable, or from the perspective of relativism, a belief in a larger absolute is also inevitable. As a result, the concepts of nihilism and relativism give meaning and absolution necessity.

Ultimately, if meaning is cyclical it implies that it is infinite, but if this infinite meaning can be regulated into concepts (as can be compared to the colour spectrum, or musical circle of fourths or fifths), it implies that the infinite is structured. As argued however, the structure of something that is infinite is paradoxical as it would ordain both meaning and opposition to meaning. What it does demonstrate however is that infinity is an ideal form only comprehendible as a pure concept. However, as contrast and infinity are so fundamental to meaning, to consider them as only constructs of the mind would jeopardise any notion of existence altogether. For example, how could existence be thought of as finite? What would replace the finite when it was finished? Any new state would imply a new space and time to continue the infinite. Inversely however, to imply a state of no space and time is also to imply an infinite nothingness. Infinity must be idealistic as well as being implicated in the fabric and grand pattern of existence. Therefore, there must be more to contrast and indeterminacy than meets the eye, as contrast is the only thing that allows us to make sense of what would otherwise be meaningless chaos.

**Table IV-6**

---

**Chapter Summary:**
- Life is both common to and distinct from observable physics, as it can only be seen in the contrast between observations.
- Life is not exclusive to either mind or body. It is not possible to isolate life to either one.
- The human and the spirit (or something akin to either two) are intractable from subjectivity, but at the same time may not be seen as total or absolute.
- The contrast between the human and nature is abundantly productive of meaning and narrative.
- Evolutionary theory as deterministic is a partial narrative.
- Necessity is not absolute; all concepts should not be reduced to necessity alone. Such a stance should not be considered as delegitimising, but in fact is the basis of legitimising facets of society, nature etc.

---

# Endnotes

[1] Such as Spinoza's (1996) understanding of substance; or Deleuze's (2001) understanding of difference.

[2] Despret (2017) discusses the presence of those who have passed away in eyes of those who remember the deceased and considers what this means for philosophy.

[3] The term cartesian anxiety is termed by Bernstein (1983).

[4] The soul and spirit may seem too similar to contrast, but their opposition has some coverage in Oswald Spengler (1980). The soul governs the personal aspects of an individual e.g. ego, while the spirit governs the impersonal, universal, heavenly component.

[5] David Chalmers (2017) introduces the zombie into philosophy of mind.

[6] For example see Levinas (1969), who broadly inspired a generation of French thought when arguing how the 'I' of first principles obscures a more embracive view of the other. Also see Foucault (2001a), who argues that humanism and enlightenment exist in a state of tension: as humanism sought to establish norms, Enlightenment thought attempted to transcend all that is material, including the boundaries that are constructed by humanistic thought.

[7] There is much evidence to point to thought systems that do not rely on a contrast to understand mind that is not against body, for example Indian chakras and the Chinese Xin contrast mind more evidently with emotion.

8 "But truly to escape Hegel involves an exact appreciation of the price we have to pay to detach ourselves from him. It assumes that we are aware of the extent to which Hegel, insidiously perhaps, is close to us; it implies a knowledge, in that which permits us to think against Hegel, of that which remains Hegelian. We have to determine the extent to which our anti-Hegelianism is possibly one of his tricks directed against us, at the end of which he stands, motionless, waiting for us." (Foucault, 1982, p. 235).

9 As a result a whole generation of philosophers has inherited an apprehension to dialectic. In recent times dialectic has some modern readings that attempt to avert interpretations of the end of history e.g. Žižek (2012) Jameson (2014).

10 This could be linked to Nietzsche's (2017) view of will. Perhaps with it could also be said that Nietzsche's shadow is equally difficult one to escape.

11 Similar to the pursuit of Object Oriented Ontology that assigns objects agency. It addresses the question of 'when does an object become an object' by demonstrating that objects stem from contradiction they are neither independent to the viewer nor totally owned by them at the same time.

12 Reminiscent of Heidegger's (2013) Dasein, being in the world.

13 This point follows the famous argument between Derrida and Foucault (2001a) on the possibility of understanding historical perspectives, and is encompassed in Foucault's method of archaeology.

14 This has implications for the way in which knowledge and epistemology are formed. If the natural sciences are said to be geared towards knowledge of nature, and the humanities and social sciences the human, the knowledge being sought here of contrast is neither. This is not to claim the distinctions are not important, on the contrary what is implied is the need to recognise a form of knowledge which is 'meta'.

15 On these grounds William James' (2007) pragmatism has gone to the extreme of challenging the 'concreteness' of the human or any species whatsoever, arguing instead that there are only really organisms. But in this view who is to say there is even organism and not just energy. It is impossible to think of evolution without some sort of contrast between the human, species, nature and other organisms and animals.

16 Something of which he was acutely aware of: "My point is not that everything is bad, but that everything is dangerous, which is not exactly the same as bad. If everything is dangerous, then we always have something to do. So my position leads not to apathy but to a hyper and pessimistic activism. I think that the ethico-political choice we have to make every day is to determine which is the main danger." (Foucault, 1991).

17 Evidence for this is overwhelming, see, The English root for so many anti-civilised concepts e.g. philistine, barbarian and vandal is from the Latin for tribes threatening Roman rule. Or in the insularity of China's golden era evidenced in the Huang-Ming Zuxun. The same sentiment can be demised from the commander of the U.S. forces in Vietnam Westmoreland quoted in the film *Hearts and Minds:* "The Oriental doesn't put the same high price on life as does a Westerner. Life is plentiful. Life is cheap in the Orient."

18 This can even be traced in philosophy as the schisms of 'analytic' philosophy being set aside from 'continental' as being linked with nationalist and ideological concerns of the two European world wars of the 20th century (Akehurst, 2011).

[19] Frisby and Sayer give an account of the modern usage of the word 'society' in its current form, the word has altered but similar concepts have been used to describe the collective or the tribe.

[20] This could be compared to the process of individuation presented by Simondon (2007). However, rather than describe it as an incomplete and ongoing process where a "pre-individual" is always left-over, here it must be understood as both incomplete and complete in that individuals must define themselves against all things outside of their individuality but that the individual can never define the exact point at where this can be located.

[21] The latest iteration in speculative materialism has attempted to find authenticity by accepting the existence of alternative accounts but does so at the expense of the authentication of the subject, choosing instead to deny the subject all together and speculate on all the unknowns of existence beyond the individual.

[22] Not to say that these uncertainties are necessarily accepted by all, or not open to interpretation, see Smolin (2019).

# Conclusion

The effect of the combining rhetoric and dialectic produces a method that ensures that nothing can be explained with one single principle alone, nor can it be explained as the balance between two dualistically contrasting principles or even the balance between a whole range of concepts (for example, even contrast has been contradicted with complementation). When searching for the balance between concepts that balance merely becomes a new singular principle, the beginnings of a new extreme, and new dualism seeking to explain or express something (the dynamics of concepts could be described as in a constant state of enantiodromia but with no state of balance).

In each of the diagrams explored no one concept can be understood in isolation. So to argue from the extremity of any one individual concept alone is an impossible position to ever fully achieve, just as the exact middle position of all the concepts in one diagram is also impossible to fully achieve. However, when in dialogue to take no position on the diagram is also impossible. In the course of any dialogue the assumption of specific positions is inevitable and unavoidable, and no position may encompass all the others, any position assumed has the potential to be contradicted (as demonstrated by Heraclitus in his understanding of logos). As a result, each and every course of action is always positioned against its own contradictory position, and this means that action and argument must always involve a choice. As in mathematical terminology, we could choose to call this contradiction irrational, however, it is just as rational as irrational (and metaphysics should have allegiance to both and therefore be irrational just as much as the rational). Every stage of dialogue has the possibility to take three alternative paths it can affirm the original concept, take a contrary stance or seek to complimentarily combine the two. This could be used to imply the primacy of dialectic or logic, but relying entirely on either recourse results in a partial view of what is going on and a concepts wider relation to meaning (e.g. results in logocentrism, first challenged by Aristotle's rhetorical demonstration of ethos and pathos as equal to logos). Choice and expression are just as important to this process as determination and positioning as meaning has no medium without a combination of both. Thought and action are always both chosen and arbitrary dictated.

Accordingly, the place of logic and reason in such an explanation has a nuanced relation to the process described above. Logic has in common one quality shared with all the things it observers, i.e. that logic relies on contrast for definition in the same way as everything else around it. Our concept of logic can never fully describe how logic itself is a 'real' thing just as in the same way our concept of anything is only ever merely a partial reflection of it. Perspective and meaning always comes from between concepts. Accepting this aspect of logic allows thought to speculate on how logic and reason exist relationally as a part of the same reality as everything else and so must reflect the world in and of itself as much as it doesn't. Therefore, concepts could be considered to be objects used to refer to other objects. However, just as their similarity allows them to be compared to the physical, there must also be something distinguishing them from other physical objects in order for them to be operational and understandable. The concepts themselves are based on the interactions between physical matter and energy and so are not the same as either but are tuned to be able to interpret in this surrounding. Logic therefore is essential and enables us to operate as part of a world that is both bigger and smaller than it (surrounding it in all dimensions). Logic and reason are therefore not inherently meaningful, they become meaningful through reflection on the juxtaposition of contrasts.

Such an approach is aiming to avoid flattening out or levelling thought. Thought becomes flattened or levelled when it is used to extremes to either divide the world into rigid immutable categories or equally to overemphasise the flexibility and relativity of categories. The most ready example of this happens between the many camps divided around attempting to debate the existence of the world itself as distinct from our interpretation of it and the world as ideal (a paradigm ever at the forefront from Plato to any single modern-day philosophical movement and impossibly nuanced). The argument here does not wish to dismiss any of the many positions possible in relation to this enquiry. Rather demonstrate how they are intricately linked, and to suggest that discussion of this intricate linkage should not begin with a premise that seeks to eliminate the contrast and contradiction that make either one meaningful. Although it is impossible to avoid taking a stance, the implication is that philosophy (and the disciplines it feeds) should avoid emphasising the flattening totalisms of any one particular monism, dualism or any other extremes in the concerns and controversies that it works towards. Rather it should consider the contrasts which have made perceivable logics meaningful even if contradictory.

If existence cannot be captured in one concept or metaphor or one particular thought, little evidence exists to describe meaning (or by extension the universe or existence) as inherently cyclical, linear, transcendent or ideal (or a square, or a hexagon, or anything else), it must be all of these things and infinitely more. Many meta-physical (and physical) distinctions can be made of properties (e.g. from Plato's theory of forms or Laozi's Dao/Tao to Jainism's anekāntavāda). The very fact that these ideal forms can be expressed at all necessitates the question of where to place them (and their respective truths and fallacies). All meaningful distinctions must have some truth even if only as a metaphor, whilst not being the entire literal truth, such literalism is impossible for subjects within the world they are trying to describe. Metaphysics at its most simply cannot avoid implying a version of how existence derives from one form that has diverged into two and from between these two forms comes to form all the rest of the forms observed. It is impossible to describe existence as exclusively in form or flux either as their meaning relies on each other for expression. In order to describe anything metaphysically or otherwise, it is essential to conceptualise both how things are never one distinct form, whilst at the same time must allude to some kind of distinct and universal form otherwise distinction would be indescribable and have no meaning. This implies that meanings are infinite and can never be fully represented with one concept alone, but at the same time concepts can never avoid implying some sort of finite meaning never fully contained in the circumstances of its utterance, pointing to the bound boundlessness and profundity of meaning.

The linear and the cyclical are joined through this explanation and describe the infinity we find in pi, Euler's constant or the golden ratio. Each of them is an exploration (as are the tables here) of what exists in the always elusive middle between whole things (the excluded middle). Each of these phenomena uses a pattern to uncover a form between 1 and 0. Such evocations of infinity demonstrate a constant direction that never reaches completion. They demonstrate how everything observed from the middle can either conglomerate or dismember but never be whole or disappear completely. Similarly, meta-physics can never bring about infinite possibility or result in infinite regress, all meaning is always suspended between the two. The more that logic is elaborated upon, the more that possibilities are closed down and vice versa. In this way philosophies always have an equal possibility to both open up concepts as much as to close them down. Even philosophies of radical becoming or non-reducibility (such as Deleuze, 2014) cannot escape the inevitability of closing concepts down. To attempt non-reducibility is the same as to commit wholly to any one principle alone. The endeavour hides the inevitability of contrast and in so doing portrays difference as supreme (at the expense of similarity), ultimately closing all other possibilities, and so resulting in an extreme partiality.

To negate the negative as anything more than difference (i.e. to deny the existence of nothing) results in a total belief in the positive (that which is posited), but this causes a contradiction as to believe in the positive must actually mean a belief in the negative, as what is making the positive distinct other than its contrast with that which it is not? And as nothing is a part of everything, to believe in nothing is to also to believe in something. This contradiction is perhaps one of the clearest examples of contrast itself. Beyond this contrast, it is difficult to assert meaning, but the history of philosophy contains some important attempts, for example: Kant would say that the difference between contradictory opposites is meaningless, whereas Hegel would argue that there is a unity of opposites between contradictions, and Nietzsche would add that there is only perspective. Rather than adopt fully any of these solutions, the metaphysical position found in this book stems from a belief in the proliferation of infinity through contrast. As in the mathematics of fractals, the space between things contains an infinity of scale, which also implies an infinity of possible forms. In the infinity of forms between contrasting objects and concepts, all of these concerns can comfortably be infinitely accommodated whilst infinitely opposed. Infinity and contrast are developed here as concepts that are impossible to distinguish between similarity and difference, singularity and non-singularity or identity and anonymity.

It could be argued that this results in an analytical perspective that is difficult to legitimise. The account here could be said to be self-defeating as there is nothing to favour the legitimisation of any meaning over its de-legitimisation. However, such a criticism also evokes the very premise of knowledge itself. The most common summation of Plato's (1987b) definition of knowledge is as justified true belief. In the 20th century, this model of knowledge was challenged by Gettier (1963) who put forward circumstances where a belief may be true and justified but not necessarily knowledge. E.g. in cases where inferences are made that turn out to be true even if the fact they were initially inferred from proves to be false. The effect of this distinction prompted many responses for the need for a fourth condition of truth, such as infallibility, defeasibility, or some other necessity. However, here this ambiguity is precisely the point, the only truth ever fully available to the individual is the truth of their belief, and the quality of this belief lies in their justification of knowledge from conjecture (demonstrating the breadth of the Socratic paradox). Therefore, knowledge is related to truth (whilst retaining its ability to be falsified), but not fully tied to the concept of truth alone without contrast.

On the one hand, knowledge could be seen as the task of creating affirmational, all-encompassing universal categories. However, on the other knowledge could also be knowing the limits of categorisation and when further categorisation is not needed. The demands of scientific culture and liberal democracy emphasise both accurate categorisation and the allowance of free association between categories. This is reflected in the polemics formed in the modern academy across its different divisions and departments. Ironically, to operate as an individual in such a regime involves the inevitability of navigating more than one totalising polemic. To think free of these polemics, or even to be able to accept their contradictions is extremely difficult, because to contradict them is to create new ones for which maybe new to the individual but is already saturated in the public consciousness. The method postulated in this book is an attempt to think around them. It both confirms the universal categories found in the tables whilst providing a way to dismiss them. In this sense, it is difficult to align with any one school of thought, rather than a weakness however, the huge possibilities for comparison are the key strength to the method. It is the key difference between this method and the absolution of mathematics or the relativism (and obscurantism) of post-modernism philosophies or from the dogma of theology, mysticism and religion. The method given here gives concepts a root and form that is affirmed and disaffirmed in the recursive self-validation of their opposition.

The advantage of charting concepts with contrast (rather than logic or reason) is to avoid the understanding of any one particular concept as prescient, and to display what further concepts they conceive. Therefore, logic and reason may be inevitable to reflection but are not essential to meaning. If meaning is infinite it implies that there is no end to any one meanings nuance. So much attention in metaphysics is spent on logic, as if logic accounts entirely for metaphysics as well as physics. When logic is over-emphasised, it is assumed to be an end in itself rather than a guide to that which is beyond it and of which it is a part of. Logic only forms one part of thought as thought is accessible to all the senses. Thought is linked to and closely interlinked with sense, feeling and mood. It is impossible to contain all thought as occurring in just one place. Thought must exist between many interlinked looping relays between reflection, feeling and outside contrasts.

Thought (and feeling) emanate from contrast and are related to the forms and structures shared between energy and matter, but thought is also distinct from both energy and matter and can be seen to inverse (contrast) the properties of that which is perceived as matter or energy. A thought (or feeling) comprises the transformation of energy from one physical manifestation to the next, in a reaction that becomes more and more internalised into cells, nerves and neurons until it becomes self-reflexive. The thought (or feeling) is therefore, neither the matter, nor the energy, but makes up its own third thing, neither fully one, or the other. This has a big implication for philosophy because thought and concepts can be seen as both physical and metaphysical at the same time. Whereas the question of this kind have mainly been framed around empiricism and its limitations, i.e. around the senses and what one can and cannot sense, the method here focuses on the concepts (and contrasts) and not solely on the physical senses, and as a result, the question is turned around. Analysis here attempts to look outward from the concept to the senses rather than the other way around. Here the method uses contrast to reflect upon the concept, where no other inference is required. Even though thought is just another kind of sense, tracing oppositional concepts allows for an insight into the mechanisms required for thoughts to function. It could be argued that the results of which can only ever provide insight into the relational dynamics of an individual's understanding of a concept and not the 'actual' things that comprises that concept. However, as contrast is so fundamental to thought, if there was no correlation between the contrast felt in a thought and the dynamics of contrast used to sense wider existence, there would be no point to thought thinking about existence, or to think in general. Such a trail of thought provokes the question as to why would such beings as ourselves exist in a state so unrelated to the world around us? The very contrast of our inner thinking selves to the exterior meaningfulness of the world is perhaps the strongest proof of each of their interrelated existences.

### Table V-1

The meaning of every concept on the tables made throughout this book implies a sequence that cannot be understood without some alternate means of organisation which pre-programs the pattern. I have mitigated this with a notion of contrast, or difference that is neither a priori nor entirely a posterior to meaning. However, any search for an origin poses a real danger and any such attempt should understandably evoke some controversy given the contestation of the subject and the lessons from history associated with a similar motive. In light of this therefore, I deemed it important to highlight some of the unanswered questions the method left me with:

- Are there some relations between concepts unaccounted for in the method, i.e. how do the tables specifically relate to one another?
- How does connotation account for differences in meaning. Especially the slight differences between different languages or the changes that occur over time? Is connotation oppositional or non-oppositional?
- At what point can it be said that a concept is singular or the combination of other concepts? Are some concepts the result of one or more concept combined? At what point would a combined concept be able to form a different spectrum?
- What can be used to test the exactitude of my hypothesis of the recursions in meaning? Is there some inherent explanation for this? Is there a relation between this and our other senses of things like musical scales? Or the colour wheel?

\*\*\*

The method proposed here is not designed to oppose or compliment any one particular epistemology or science (or denounce or demote in any way).

Instead, the focus is on concepts and their opposites, but from this pretence many once incompatible epistemes may come into contact in new ways. More specifically, the approach challenges the meanings by which scientific methodologies are interpreted and foundered. There is no predisposition of scientific method that dictates all objects under observations must be consistent, such an assumption would be biased (examples can be found in the failure of the philosophy of Nature). Rather contradiction is the predilect of philosophy and logic since the time of Aristotle. Moreover, science provides plenty of famous examples of inconsistencies such as the Möbius strip, Schrodinger's cat or Heisenberg's uncertainty principle etc. At its most fundamental, scientific method is a means of observation and all observation rely on contrast for expression. This means that science should not dictate or assume objects or the boundaries of objects without observation. Rather objects are saying as much about the form of contrast as they are about their own form. This represents a shift in focus but once conceived in this way, science can already be seen as a means to view contrast more directly. It is when the results of science or philosophy are interpreted as a means to an end, that sooner or later end in distortion.

The rhetoric/dialectic method used throughout this book employs scepticism in a similar way to the scientific method. For example, the assertion of opposition can be said to be the essence of scepticism. The method forwarded here is one with long linages in scepticism, but one aware of the cyclicality of belief and able to foreground traditions such as stoicism v Epicureanism (to be independent of internal influences) or a secularism that accounts for rationalism v fideism (to be independent of external influences) with an aim to allow thought to be as independent as possible from all possible biases (the effort to find first principles). As such, scepticism relates to belief and experience and is placed between naivety/trivialism (a belief in everything) and cynicism (a belief in nothing). Scepticism would be a perspective in-between these two extremes (avoiding dogmatism and criticism as is detailed in Kant). To assert that scepticism implies rationalism alone (as promulgated in enlightenment) is a radicalisation of scepticism that takes it to an idealised (teleological) extreme to exclude all 'non-rational' experiences. Rationalism asserts a burden of proof upon nature (as rationalism sees reason as the prime force of nature), the method used in this book deprioritises both subject and objects altogether following only their contrast (even unto being sceptical of scepticism). Rather than result in incoherence the circle loops back upon itself and is proof of something external (to both the human and nature) becomes difficult to deny. Regardless of perspective or theoretical lens, belief and narrative (both collective and individual) are recognised as something inevitable.

Philosophy or science envisaged as a means to isolate and strip concepts of belief are destined to hypocrisy. For example, such motives hold no shortage of belief in progress, wellbeing and security that relies upon a dialectic working towards one particular ideology. Recent history is hard to decipher without these narratives, for example, the 20th century is interpreted by its grand ideologies and then the cold war/space race and even into the 21st century environmentalism presents a similar lens to make sense of the history. The method here attempts not to separate contradictions into different camps, because to do so risks fracturing the narrative. Recent history (i.e. the so-called 'post-truth' era) has been typified as one where collective values and beliefs have become more diffuse and dispersed at the expense of societal cohesion. Nietzsche's (1974) 'will to power' is the most pronounced in a long tradition in idealism to perceive the dangers of disperse beliefs and stress the importance to assert common values. After the atrocities of the 20th century however, accounts of this type have been heavily opposed. As a result, less attention has focused on how a society with diffused values and beliefs already forms an ideology (even if inevitable Badiou, 2012; 2019). Therefore, rather than continuing to imagine dialectic as one unifying force, it should be imagined as containing exception for any one ideology alone. To collectivise with a multitude of ideologies is quite a feat as from the point of view of the individual it is an illogical position to maintain. Yet from the point of view of history, this tolerance to multiple belief is the project the current epoch is charged with whilst all the while acutely aware of environmental catastrophe and our species' inevitable demise (see Danowski and Castro, 2016 for a demonstration on how this may already be taking place). Rather than the end of history as prophesied by Hegel (and much feared and derided) being the endpoint of socio-economic evolution, perhaps the challenge was always to create a contradictory humanity tolerant to inconsistency in belief yet able to provide a sustainable direction for life collectively (Jenkins, 2003). Contemporary concerns such as environmentalism or global health and wellbeing pose such challenges as their solution must be all-embracing on the one hand whilst being voluntary on the other (as environmentalism that is mandatory is harder to justify as environmentalism should give equal will to all parts of the environment). Such a project is futile if done whilst seeing life and meaning fatalistically. As such, every perspective on humanity (current and historic) has a utopia just as it has a dystopia, narrative is recursive unto an never-ending minutiae of meanings, it is their contrast with what is indeterminable that makes them meaningful, yet always fated to be surpassed.

In all this, what necessity are the natural sciences if not contrasted and complimented by philosophy, and vice versa. In such contrast, concepts such as humanity or society are made meaningful and rely on science for coherence. Any attempt to resolve contrasts between science and philosophy should be mindful of the productiveness of the contrast between each account. For example, biological racism, eugenics, phrenology are all concepts first conceived scientifically that later became pseudoscience. As a result, these concepts now hold little value for the natural sciences. However, for philosophy, they continue to be of the utmost importance, and as a case studies still actively have a role in the demarcation of the discipline. Successive works of the humanities or social sciences continue to disavow these concepts, yet even the hardiest philosophical position struggles to justify its disavowal without the examples provided by science.

The point therefore, is not only on how to demarcate disciplines or regimes as all demarcation leads to is further demarcation, rather it is also about how disciplines are necessitated comparatively. Rather than believing in ideals as binaries attempting to judge right from wrong they must be judged as ways to work out meaning from purpose. However, this is a difficult balance to maintain as trying to find meaning in everything will result in only finding non-sense, and trying too hard to isolate meaning will only result in too much self-sensitivity. Similarly, the result of too much reason in any direction (science, humanities and social sciences included) results in meaninglessness. For example, if the whole world is reasonable there is no such thing as reason, or if the whole world is science then science would be indistinguishable from the whole world, or if all the world were disenchanted (or enchanted) then disenchantment (or enchantment) would be the world. Their uniqueness would be impossible to sense or contemplate as the sense of them derives from their contrast.

What does this say then about purpose? The question continues to hold an age-old anxiety, as we don't actually have to do anything, and anything we choose to do is subject to resistance, yet we inhabit a world where it is impossible to do nothing. So the real tragedy is meaninglessness, but meaninglessness can only be understood fleetingly as meaninglessness evokes more meaning and our perspective becomes caught between the two. Thoughts only alternative to think beyond meaning or meaninglessness is from the middle, therefore it is always possible to imagine further eventualities as meaninglessness in this instance still means something even as a contrast to whatever means something now. Even if existence were to mean nothing, meaning has existed meaning that there is no such all eternal meaningless nothing without infinite contrast. This highlights a prime quality of meaning, that it must self-refer in order to be meaningful, implying that it is in an infinite loop encompassing the internal personal world to the external cosmos. Meaning that does not lead back onto itself, instantly becomes meaningless or non-sensical. The real profundity of this position is that without the existence of the meaninglessness meaning cannot exist.

The purpose of existence is the purpose of purpose itself. Similarly, the meaning of life is to make meaning (see Frankl, 2004). Singular concepts such as will, reason, purpose, necessity or absolution cannot convey meaning on their own without distortion. The task of philosophy should be considered as a means to maintain the distinctions between meanings without allowing one singular meaning to dominate all others, and some caution should be held the use of philosophy oblivious to this responsibility. E.g. will, reason, purpose, necessity and absolution should never come to mean the same thing. Although contrast remains a concept like any other and should not be taken to mean everything, its use as a metaphor is inherently useful to help to achieve the task of distinction. Viewing the contrast behind making sense allows for a perspective that simultaneously links the individual to the collective, and the animate to the inanimate, voluntary to the involuntary, weaving together meaning with what contrasts and opposes it. Contrast adjudicates not only the momentary interpretations of the here and now, but is also contrasted against larger narratives by which a subject will be valued, and collectives value themselves by. Such juridical actions can be found in the everyday activity of playing a sport, making art, law abidance, being fashionable. Collectively these activities constitute not only the individual but also the society, and the worlds we place ourselves within. In this way, the categories inevitably create universal forms, whilst also only ever being personal forms to the subject. In the infinite contrast between substance form abounds infinitely, and even the most familiar of forms are merely aggregates onto which there is an unceasing level of specific detail to be found within. Contrast can never omit that which it excludes entirely, and any consideration of contrast contains its own exception within. This means that rather than assuming that the exclusion of contrast results in the real, it is time to re-evaluate the inevitability of contrast and its role in regulating thought away from extremes, not just towards them. If the world we inherit cannot be said to be either entirely meaningful or meaningless, rather than lament the peremptory existence unto which we are thrust, it is of the greatest importance that we realise that it is this very fact allows us the ongoing chance to embrace meaning.

# References

Akehurst, T. L. (2011). *The Cultural Politics of Analytic Philosophy: Britishness and the spectre of Europe*. London: Bloomsbury Publishing.

Althusser, L. (2005). *For Marx* (B. Brewster, Trans.). London: Verso.

Arendt, H. (2017). *The origins of totalitarianism*. London: Penguin Classics.

Ariès, P. (1982). *The Hour of Our Death*. New York: Vintage Books.

Aristotle. (1889). *The Organon, Or Logical Treatises, of Aristotle: with Introduction of Porphyry* (O. F. Owen, Trans.). London: G. Bell.

Aristotle. (1996). *Poetics* (M. Heath, Trans.). London: Penguin Classics.

Aristotle. (1998). *The Metaphysics* (H. C. Lawson-Tancred, Trans.). London: Penguin Classics.

Aristotle. (2012). *The Art of Rhetoric*. London: Collins Classics.

Arneson, P. (Ed.). (2007). *Perspective on Philosophy of Communication*. West Lafayette Indiana: Purdue University Press.

Arnett, R. C. (2012). *Communication Ethics in Dark Times: Hannah Arendt's Rhetoric of Warning and Hope*. Carbondale, Ill: Southern Illinois University Press.

Arnett, R. C. & Holba, A. M. (2012). *An Overture to Philosophy of Communication: The carrier of meaning*. New York: Peter Lang Publishing.

Ayer, A. J. (1991). *The Central Questions of Philosophy*. London: Penguin.

Azzouni, J. (2003). The Strengthened Liar, the Expressive Strength of Natural Languages, and Regimentation. *The Philosophical Forum 34* (3–4), pp. 329–350. [https://doi.org/10.1111/1467-9191.00142]

Baars, B. J. (1988). *A Cognitive Theory of Consciousness*. Cambridge: Cambridge University Press.

Badiou, A. (2012). *The Rebirth of History: Times of Riots and Uprisings*. London: Verso Books.

Badiou, A. & Tusa, G. (2019). *The End: A conversation* (R. Mackay, Trans.). Cambridge: Polity.

Barad, K. (2007). *Meeting the University Halfway: quantum physics and the entanglement of matter and meaning*. Durham: Duke University Press.

Barthes, R. (2009). *Mythologies* (A. Lavers, Trans.). London: Vintage Classics.

Bataille, G. (1990). Hegel, Death and Sacrifice (J. Strauss, Trans.). *Yale French Studies 78*, pp. 9–28. [https://doi.org/10.2307/2930112]

Baudrillard, J. (1994). *Simulacra and Simulation* (S. F. Glaser, Trans.). Ann Arbor: The University of Michigan Press.

Bauman, Z. (1991). *Modernity and the Holocaust*. Cambridge: Polity Press.

Becker, E. (1985). *The Denial of Death*. New York: The Free Press/Macmillan.

Benjamin, W. (2015). *Illuminations* (H. Zorn, Trans.). London: the Bodley Head.

Bergson, H. (1999). *Duration and Simultaneity: Bergson and the Einsteinian Universe* (R. Durie, Trans.). Manchester: Clinamen Press.

Bergson, H. (2014). *Time and Free Will: An Essay on the Immediate Data of Consciousness* (F. L. Pogson, Trans.). London: Routledge.

Bernstein, L. (1990). *The Unanswered Question: Six Talks at Harvard: (Charles Eliot Norton Lectures)*, Cambridge, Massachusetts: Harvard University Press.

Bernstein, R. J. (1983). *Beyond objectivism and relativism: science, hermeneutics, and praxis.* Philadelphia: University of Philadelphia Press.

Berthoz, A. (2009). *Emotion and reason: the cognitive science of decision making.* Oxford: Oxford University Press.

Bostrom, N. (2003). Are You Living in a Computer Simulation? *Philosophical Quarterly 53* (211), pp. 243–253.

Braidotti, R. (2013). *The Posthuman.* Cambridge: Polity Press.

Brassier, R. (2013). That Which Is Not: Philosophy as Entwinement of Truth and Negativity. *Stasis 1*, pp. 174–186.

Brassier, R. (2007). *Nihil Unbound: Enlightenment and Extinction.* Basingstoke: Palgrave Macmillan.

Brassier, R., Hamilton Grant, I., Harman, G. & Meillassoux, Q. (2007). Speculative Realism (pp. 307–450). In Mackay, R. (Ed.), *Collapse: Unknown Deleuze: Volume 3.* Falmouth: Urbanomic.

Braver, L. (2007). *A Thing of This World: A History of Continental Anti-realism.* Evanston, Illinois: Northwestern University Press.

Breazeale, D. (2014). Against Nature? On the Status and Meaning of the Natural World in J. G. Fichte's early Wissenschaftslehre. *Metafusica 45*, pp. 185–205. [https://doi.org/info:doi/10.18910/51525]

Bryant, L., Srnicek, N. & Harman, G. (2010). *The Speculative Turn: Continental materialism and realism.* Victoria: re.press.

Burbidge, J. (2007). *Hegel's Systematic Contingency.* Basingstoke: Palgrave Macmillan.

Burckhardt, M. Höfer, D. (2017). *All and Nothing: a digital apocalypse.* London: Verso.

Butchart, G. C. (2019). *Embodiment, Relation, Community: A Continental Philosophy of Communication.* University Park, Pennsylvania: Penn State University Press.

Campbell, J. (1989). *The Power of Myth.* New York: Bantam Doubleday Dell Publishing Group.

Carnap, R. (1932). The Elimination of Metaphysics Through Logical Analysis of Language (A. Pap Trans.). *Erkenntnis* pp. 60–81.

Catt, I.E. (2014). The Two Sciences of Communication in Philosophical Context. *Review of Communication 14* (3–4), pp. 201–228.

Chalmers, D. (1995). Facing Up to the Problem of Consciousness. *Journal of Consciousness Studies 2* (3), pp. 200–219.

Chalmers, D. (2017). Zombies on the Web – David Chalmers. URL http://consc.net/zombies-on-the-web/ (accessed 6.25.19).

Chang, B. G. & Butchart, G. C. (2012). *Philosophy of Communication.* Cambridge, Massachusetts: MIT Press.

Chase, S. (1966). *The Tyranny of Words.* San Diego: HBJ Book Publishers.

Chomsky, N. (2010). Some Simple Evo Devo Theses: how true might they be for language? In Larson, R. K. (Ed.), *The Evolution of Human Language: Biolinguistic Perspectives* (pp.45–63). Cambridge: Cambridge University Press.

Christias, D. (2016). Sellars, Meillassoux, and the Myth of the Categorial Given in advance: A Sellarian Critique of "Correlationism" and Meilassoux's "Speculative Realism." *Journal of Philosophical Research 41* pp. 105-128. [https://doi.org/10.5840/jpr201662970]

Clemens, J. (2013). Vomit Apocalypse; Or, Quentin Meillassoux's After Finitude. *Parrhessia 18*, pp. 57–67.

Collingwood, R. G. (1960). *The Idea of Nature.* Oxford: Oxford University Press.

Crick, F. & Koch, C. (1990). Towards a neurobiological theory of consciousness. *Seminars in the Neurosciences.* 2, pp. 263–275.

Cruse, D. A. (2001). *Lexical Semantics.* Cambridge: Cambridge University Press.

Damasio, A. R. (2006). *Descartes' Error: emotion, reason and the human brain.* London: Vintage.

Danowski, D. Castro, E. V. (2016). *The Ends of the World.* Cambridge: Polity Press.

Darwin, C. (2018). *The Expression of the Emotions in Man and Animals.* Mineola, New York: Dover Publications.

Darwin, C. (1871). *The Descent of Man.* New York: D. Appleton and Company.

Davies, M. (2014). *Oppositions and Ideology in news discourse.* London: Bloomsbury Press.

De Man, P. (1996). *Allegories of Reading: figural language in Rousseau, Nietzsche, Rilke, and Proust.* New Haven: Yale University Press.

Deleuze, G. (2014). *Difference and Repetition.* London: Bloomsbury Press.

Deleuze, G. (2001). *Pure Immanence: Essays on a life* (A. Boyman, Trans.). New York: Zone Books.

Deleuze, G. & Guattari, F. (1983). *Capitalism and Schizophrenia.* Minneapolis: University of Minnesota Press.

Dennett, D. C. (2007). *Breaking the Spell: religion as a natural phenomenon.* London: Penguin.

Derrida, J. (2017). *Dissemination* (B. Johnson Trans.). Chicago: University of Chicago Press.

Derrida, J. (2016). *Of Grammatology* (G. C. Spivak, Trans.). Baltimore: Johns Hopkins University Press.

Descartes, R. (2008). *Meditations on First Philosophy: with selections from the Objections and replies* (M. Moriarty Trans.). Oxford: Oxford University Press.

Descola, P. (2013). *Beyond Nature and Culture.* Chicago: University of Chicago Press.

Despret, V. (2017). *Au Bonheur des Morts: Récits de ceux qui restent.* Paris: Éditions La Découverte.

Dick, P. K. (1988). *I hope I Shall Arrive Soon.* London: Grafton.

Dilthey, W. (2010). *Wilhelm Dilthey: Selected Works, Volume IV: Hermeneutics and the Study of History.* Princeton: Princeton University Press.

Durkheim, E. (2014). *The Rules of Sociological Method: And selected texts on sociology and its method* (S. Lukes, Trans.). New York: Simon and Schuster.

Edmonds, D. & Eidinow, J. (2001). *Wittgenstein's Poker: The story of a ten-minute argument between two great philosophers.* London: Faber and Faber.

Eemeren, F. H. V. & Houtlosser P (Eds.) (2002). *Dialectic and Rhetoric: The warp and woof of argumentation analysis.* New York: Springer.

Egginton, W., Sandbothe, M. (Eds.) (2004). *The Pragmatic Turn in Philosophy: Contemporary engagements between analytic and continental thought.* Albany: State University of New York Press.

Estrada-Gonzalez, L. (2012). Models of Possibilism and Trivialism. *Logic and Logical Philosophy.* 21 (2), pp. 175–205. [http://dx.doi.org/10.12775/LLP.20 12.010]

Eysenck, H. J. (2000). *The psychology of politics.* London: Routledge.

Feyerabend, P. (1993). *Against Method.* London: Verso.

Fichte, J. G. (2000). *Foundations of Natural Right* (F. Neuhouser, Trans.). Cambridge: Cambridge University Press.

Foucault, M. (2001a). *The Order of Things.* London: Routledge.

Foucault, M. (2001b). *Dits et Ecrits, tome 2: 1976 - 1988.* Paris: Gallimard.

Foucault, M. (1991). On the Genealogy of Ethics: An overview of work in progress (P. Rabinow, trans.). In Rabinow, P. (Ed.). *The Foucault Reader* (pp. 340–373). London: Penguin Books.

Foucault, M. (1982). *The Archaeology of Knowledge and the Discourse on Language* (A. Sheridan Trans.). New York: Pantheon.

Foucault, M. (1977). *Discipline and Punish: The Birth of the Prison* (A. Sheridan Trans.). London: Penguin.

Frankl, V. E. (2004). *Man's Search for Meaning: The classic tribute to hope from the Holocaust.* London: Random House.

Frazer, J. G. (2009). *The Golden Bough a Study in Magic and Religion.* Oxford: Oxford University Press.

Freud, S. (2003). *The Uncanny* (D. McLintock, Trans.). London: Penguin.

Fuentes, A. (2017). *The Creative Spark: How imagination made humans exceptional.* New York: Dutton.

Gabriel, M. (2017). *Why the world does not exist* (G. Moss, Trans.). Cambridge: Polity Press.

Gadamer, H. G. (2004). *Truth and Method* (J Weinsheimer, Trans.). London: Continuum.

Gadamer, H.G., (1975). Hermeneutics and Social Science. Cult. *Hermeneutics* 2, pp. 307–316. [https://doi.org/10.1177/019145377500200402]

Garcia, T. (2014). *Form and Object: A Treatise on Things.* Edinburgh: Edinburgh University Press.

Garis, H. D. (2005). *The Artilect War: Cosmists Vs. Terrans: A bitter controversy concerning whether humanity should build godlike massively intelligent machines.* Palm Springs: ETC Publications.

Gettier, E. L. (1963). Is Justified True Belief Knowledge? *Analysis 23*, pp. 121–123. [https://doi.org/10.1093/analys/23.6.121]

Gödel, K. (1986). On formally undecidable propositions of Principia Mathematica and related systems I, in: Feferman, S. (Ed.), *Collected Works. / Vol. I.* Oxford: Oxford University Press.

Goffman, E. (1968). *Stigma: Notes on the management of spoiled identity.* London: Penguin.

Golumbia, D. (2016). "Correlationism": The Dogma that Never Was. *Bound 2* (43). pp. 1–25. [https://doi.org/10.1215/01903659-3469889]

Greene, B. (2000). *The Elegant Universe: Superstrings, Hidden Dimensions and the Quest for the Ultimate Theory.* London: Vintage.

Gunkel, D. J. (2007). *Thinking Otherwise: Philosophy, Communication, Technology.* West Lafayette, Indiana: Purdue University Press.

Hahn, S. S. (2007). *Contradiction in Motion: Hegel's organic concept of life and value.* Ithaca, New York: Cornell University Press.

Hallward, P. (2011). Anything is Possible: A Reading of Quentin Meillassoux's After Finitude. In Bryant, L.R., Srnicek, N., Harman, G. (Eds.), *The Speculative Turn: Continental Materialism and Realism* (pp.130–141). Victoria: re.press.

Hamilton, W., Mansel, H.L. & Veitch, J. (1860). *Lectures on metaphysics and logic.* Edinburgh and London: William Blackwood and Sons.

Han, B. C. (2018). *The Expulsion of the Other: Society, perception and communication today.* Cambridge: Polity Press.

Haraway, D. (1991). *Simians, Cyborgs and Women: The reinvention of nature.* London: Free Association Books.

Haraway, D. (1988). Situated Knowledges: The Science Question in Feminism and the Privilege of Partial Perspective. *Feminist. Studies 14* (3) pp. 575–599.

Harman, G. (2018). *Object-Oriented Ontology: a new theory of everything.* London: Pelican.

Harman, G. (2016). *Immaterialism: Objects and Social Theory.* Cambridge: Polity Press.

Harman, G. (2011). *The Quadruple Object.* Alresford: Zero Books.

Hegel, G. W. F. (2015). *Encyclopaedia of the Philosophical Sciences in Basic Outline. Part 1* (K Brinkmann & D. O. Dahlstrom Trans.). Cambridge: Cambridge University Press.

Hegel, G. W. F. (2004). *Hegel's Philosophy of Nature: Being Part Two of the Encyclopaedia of the Philosophical Sciences* (A. V. Miller Trans.). Oxford: Clarendon Press.

Hegel, G. W. F. (1976). *Phenomenology of Spirit* (A. V. Miller Trans.) Oxford: Oxford University Press.

Hegel, G. W. F. (1967). *Hegel's Philosophy of Right.* Oxford: Oxford University Press.

Heidegger, M. (1997). *Kant and the Problem of Metaphysics* (R. Taft, Trans.). Bloomington, Indiana: Indiana University Press.

Heidegger, M. (2013). *Being and Time* (J. Macquarrie & E. Robinson Trans.). Malden: Blackwell.

Heller-Roazen, D. (2017). *No One's Ways: An essay on infinite naming.* New York: Zone Books.

Heller-Roazen, D. (2007). *The Inner Touch: Archaeology of a Sensation.* New York: Zone Books.

Horkheimer, M. Adorno, T. W. (2002). *Dialectic of Enlightenment* (G. Schmitt-Noerr, Trans.). Redwood City California: Stanford University Press.

Hui, Y. (2019). *Recursivity and Contingency*. London: Rowman & Littlefield International.

Hui, Y. (2016). *On the Existence of Digital Objects*. Minneapolis: University of Minnesota Press.

Hume, D. (2008). *An enquiry concerning human understanding*. Oxford: Oxford University Press.

Hume, D. (2004). *Treatise of human nature*. London: Penguin Classics.

Ingold, T. (2016). *Lines: A Brief History*. London: Routledge.

James, W. (2015). *The Will To Believe: And Other Essays In Popular Philosophy, And Human Immortality*. New York: Dover Publications.

James, W. (2011). What is an Emotion. In Shook, J.R. (Ed.), *The Essential William James*. Amherst, New York: Prometheus Books.

James, W. (2007). Evolution and Pragmatism: An unpublished letter of William James. *The Transactions of Charles S. Peirce Society 43*, pp. 745–752.

Jameson, F. (2014). *The Hegel Variations: On the Phenomenology of Spirit*. London: Verso.

Jameson, F. (1991). *Postmodernism, Or, The cultural logic of late capitalism*. Durham: Duke University Press.

Jankélévitch, V. (2013). *Forgiveness*. Chicago: University of Chicago Press.

Jeffries, L. (2011). *Opposition in Discourse: The construction of oppositional meaning*. London: Bloomsbury Publishing.

Jenkins, K. (2003). *Rethinking History*. Abingdon: Routledge.

Jorion, P. (2016). *Le Dernier qui s'en va Éteint la Lumière: Essai sur l'Extinction de l'Humanité*. Paris: Fayard.

Josephson-Storm, J. A. (2017). *The Myth of Disenchantment: Magic, modernity, and the birth of the human sciences*. Chicago: University of Chicago Press.

Jung, C. G. (2014). *The Archetypes and the Collective Unconscious* (R. F. C. Hull, Trans.). London: Routledge.

Jung, C. G. (1988). *Nietzsche's "Zarathustra": Notes of the Seminar given in 1934 -1939. Two Volumes*. Princeton: Princeton University Press,

Kabay, P. (2008). *A Defence of Trivialism*. Melbourne: The University of Melbourne, PhD Thesis.

Kahn, C. H. (1982). Why Existence does not Emerge as a Distinct Concept in Greek Philosophy. In Morewedge, P. (Ed.), *Philosophies of Existence Ancient and Medieval*. New York: Fordham University Press.

Kant, I. (2008). *Groundwork for the Metaphysics of Morals* (M. J. Gregor, Trans.). Cambridge: Cambridge University Press.

Kant, I. (2007). *Critique of pure reason* (M. Muller & M. Weigelt, Trans.). London: Penguin Classics.

Kant, I. (2001). *Prolegomena to Any Future Metaphysics: and the Letter to Marcus Herz, February 1772* (J. W. Ellington, Trans.). Indianapolis: Hackett Publishing Company.

Kastrup, B. (2019). *The Idea of the World: A multi-disciplinary argument for the mental nature of reality*. Winchester, UK; Washington, USA: Iff Books.

Kierkegaard, S. (2013). *Fear and Trembling and the Sickness Unto Death* (A. Hannay, Trans.). Princeton: Princeton University Press.

Korzybski, A. (1933). *Science and Sanity: an introduction to non-Aristotelian systems and general semantics*, Forest Hills NY: Institute of General Semantics.

Koyre, A. (2016). *From the Closed World to the Infinite Universe*. Kettering: Angelico Press.

Krauss, L. M. (2014). *A Universe from Nothing: Why there is something rather than nothing*. New York: Atria Books.

Kripke, S. A. (2015). *Naming and Necessity*. Malden: Blackwell Publishing.

Kuhn, T. (1970). *The Structure of Scientific Revolutions*, Chicago: University of Chicago Press.

Labinger, J. A. & Collins, H. (Eds.), (2001). *The One Culture?: A Conversation about Science*. Chicago: University of Chicago Press.

Lagasnerie, G. (2012). *La Dernière Leçon de Michel Foucault: Sur le Néolibéralisme, la Théorie et la Politique*. Paris: Fayard.

Lakatos, I. (1968). Criticism and the Methodology of Scientific Research Programmes. *Proceedings of the Aristotelian Society 69*, pp. 149–186.

Lakoff, G. & Johnson, M. (1981). *Metaphors We Live By. Chicago*: University of Chicago Press.

Land, N. (2018). *Fanged Noumena: Collected Writings 1987–2007*. Falmouth: Urbanomic.

Lanigan, R. L. (2010). Theoretical and Applied Aspects of Communicology. In Wasik, Z. (Ed.), *Consultant Assembly III: In Search of Innovatory Subjects for Language and Culture Courses* (pp.7–32). Wroclaw, Poland: Philological School of Higher Education in Wroclaw Publishing.

Laruelle, F. (2017a). *Principles of Non-Philosophy* (N. Rubczak & A. P. Smith, trans.) London: Bloomsbury Publishing.

Laruelle, F. (2017b). *Anti-Badiou: on the Introduction of Maoism into Philosophy* (A. P. Smith, Trans.). London: Bloomsbury Publishing.

Latour, B. (1993). *We Have Never Been Modern* (C. Porter, Trans.). Cambridge, Massachusetts: Harvard University Press.

Leibniz, G.W. (1890a). The Monadology (G. M. Duncan, Trans.). In Duncan, G.M. (Ed.), *The Philosophical Works of Leibnitz* (pp. 218–231). New Haven: Tuttle and Co.

Leibniz, G.W. (1890b). Principles of Nature and Grace (G. M. Duncan, Trans.). In Duncan, G.M. (Ed.), *The Philosophical Works of Leibnitz* (pp. 209–217). New Haven: Tuttle and Co.

Levinas, E. (1969). *Totality and Infinity: An essay on exteriority* (A. Lingis, Trans.). Pittsburgh: Duquesne University Press.

Locke, J. (1998). *An Essay Concerning Human Understanding*, London: Penguin Classics.

Lucas, J. R. (1961). Minds, Machines and Gödel. *Philosophy 36*, pp. 112–127.

Mabille, B. (2013). *Hegel: L'épreuve de la Contingence*. Paris: Hermann.

Mack, P. (1993). *Renaissance Argument: Valla and Agricola in the Traditions of Rhetoric and Dialectic*. New York & Leiden: Brill.

Makkreel, R. (2015). *Orientation and Judgment in Hermeneutics*. Chicago: University of Chicago Press.

Malabou, C. (2016). *Before Tomorrow: Epigenesis and Rationality* (C. Shread, Trans.). Cambridge: Polity Press.

Man, P. de, (2013). *Blindness and Insight: Essays in the rhetoric of contemporary criticism*. London: Routledge.

Mandelbrot, B. (1967). How Long is the Coast of Britain? Statistical self-similarity and fractional dimension. *Science 156* (3775), pp. 636–538. [https://doi:10.1126/science.156.3775.636]

Mangion, C. (2011). *Philosophical Approaches to Communication*. Bristol: Intellect Ltd.

Mannheim, K. (2015). *Ideology And Utopia: An Introduction to the Sociology of Knowledge*. Mansfield Centre: Martino Fine Books.

Margolis, D. & Laurence, S. (2015). *The Conceptual Mind: new directions in the study of concepts*. Cambridge: MIT Press.

Maturana, H.R &, Varela, F.J. (1979). *Autopoiesis and Cognition: The Realization of the Living*. Dordrecht: D. Reidel Publishing Company.

Mayr, E. (1961). Cause and Effect in Biology: Kinds of causes, predictability, and teleology are viewed by a practicing biologist. *Science 134* (3489), pp. 1501–1506. [https://doi.org/10.1126/science.134.3489.1501]

McDougall, W. (1909). *An Introduction to Social Psychology*. London: Methuen.

McLuhan, M. (2001). *Understanding media: The extensions of man*. London: Routledge.

Meillassoux, Q. (2012). *Iteration, Reiteration, Repetition: A speculative analysis of the meaningless sign* (R. Mackay, Trans.). Unpublished Manuscript.

Meillassoux, Q. (2009). *After Finitude: An Essay on the Necessity of Contingency* (R. Brassier, Trans.). London: Bloomsbury Publishing.

Meinong, A., (1960). On the Theory of Objects (Translation of "Über Gegenstandstheorie", 1904). In Chisholm, R. (Ed.), *Realism and the Background of Phenomenology* (pp. 76–117). Glencoe, Illinois: The Free Press of Glencoe.

Merleau-Ponty, M. (1964). Eye and Mind (W. Cobb, Trans.). In Edie, J.M. (Ed.). *The Primacy of Perception: And Other Essays on Phenomenological Psychology, the Philosophy of Art, History and Politics* (pp. 159–193). Evanston Illinois: Northwestern University Press.

Mickey, S. (2016). *Coexistentialism and the Unbearable Intimacy of Ecological Emergency*. London: Lexington Books.

Monbiot, G. (2014). *Feral: Rewilding the Land, the Sea, and Human Life*. Chicago: University of Chicago Press.

Moore, G. E. (1971). *Principia Ethica*. Cambridge: Cambridge University Press.

Morin, E. (1979). *Le Paradigme Perdu: la nature humaine*. Paris: Seuil.

Morton, T., (2016). *Dark Ecology: for a logic of future coexistence*. New York: Columbia University Press.

Nagel, T. (1989). *The View from Nowhere*. Oxford: Oxford University Press.

Negarestani, R. 2018. *Intelligence and Spirit*. Falmouth: Urbanomic.

Newton, I. (1671). A letter of Mr. Isaac Newton, Professor of the Mathematicks in the University of Cambridge; containing his new theory about light and colors: sent by the author to the publisher from Cambridge, February. 6th. 1671/72; in order to be communicated to the Royal Society. *Philosophical*

*Transactions of the Royal Society of London 6*, pp. 3075–3087. https://doi. org/10.1098/rstl.1671.0072

Nietzsche, F. (2017). *The Will to Power* (M. A. Scarpitti, Tras.). London: Penguin Classics.

Nietzsche, F. (2009). *Ecce Homo* (D. Large, Trans.). Oxford: Oxford University Press.

Nietzsche, F. (2008). *The Birth of Tragedy* (D. Smith, Trans.). Oxford: Oxford University Press.

Nietzsche, F. (2003). *Beyond Good and Evil* (M. Tanner, Trans.). London: Penguin Classics.

Nietzsche, F. (1974). *Thus Spoke Zarathustra* (R. J. Hollingdale, Trans.). London: Penguin Classics.

Nolan, D. (1971). *Classifying and Analyzing Politico-Economic Systems*. San Francisco: The Individualist.

O'Banion, J. D. (1991). *Reorienting Rhetoric: The Dialectic of List and Story*. University Park: Penn State University Press.

Oizumi, M., Albantakis, L. & Tononi, G. (2014). From the Phenomenology to the Mechanisms of Consciousness: Integrated Information Theory 3.0. *PLoS Computational. Biology 10* (5). [https://doi.org/10.1371/journal.pcbi.1003588]

Osgood, C. (1964). Semantic differential technique in the comparative study of culture. *American Anthropologist 66*, pp. 171–200.

Pablé, A. (Ed.), (2017). *Critical Humanist Perspectives: The Integrational Turn in Philosophy of Language and Communication*. London: Routledge.

Padui, R. (2010). The Necessity of Contingency and the Powerlessness of Nature: Hegel's Two Senses of Contingency. *Idealistic Studies 40* (3) pp. 243–255. [https://doi.org/10.5840/idstudies201040316]

Peirce, C. S. (1976). Existential Graphs, in: Eisele, C. (Ed.), *The New Elements of Mathematics. Mathematical Miscellanea Volume III* (pp. 162–169). Hague & Atlantic Highlands, N.J: Mouton Publishers; Humanities Press.

Peirce, C. S. (1878). Illustrations of the Logic of Science VI. *In Popular Science Monthly Volume 13 August*.

Penrose, R. (1995). *Shadows of the Mind: A search for the missing science of consciousness*. London: Vintage.

Pickering, A. & Guzik, K. (2009). *The Mangle in Practice: Science, Society, and Becoming*. Durham: Duke University Press.

Pittendrigh, C. (1958). Adaptation, Natural Selection and Behavior, in A. Roe and G. G. Simpson (Eds.) *Behavior and Evolution* (pp. 390–416). New Haven: Yale University Press.

Plato, (2005). *Phaedrus* (C. Rowe, Trans.). London: Penguin Classics.

Plato, (2004). *Gorgias* (C. Emlyn-Jones, Trans.). London: Penguin Classics.

Plato, (1996). *Parmenides* (M. L. Gill & P. Ryan, Trans.). Indianapolis: Hackett Publishing.

Plato, (1987a). *The Republic* (M. Lane, trans.). London: Penguin Classics.

Plato, (1987b). *Theaetetus* (R. Waterfield, Trans.). London: Penguin Classics.

Plutchik, R. (2001). The Nature of Emotions: Human emotions have deep evolutionary roots, a fact that may explain their complexity and provide tools for clinical practice. *American Scientist 89* (4) pp. 344–350.

Popper, K. R. (2012). *The Open Society and Its Enemies.* London: Routledge.

Popper, K. R. (1974). *The Logic of Scientific Discovery,* London: Hutchinson & Co.

Popper, K. R. (1940). What is Dialectic? *Mind 49* (195) pp. 403–426.

Priest, G. (2006a). *Beyond the Limits of Thought.* Oxford: Clarendon Press.

Priest, G. (2006b). *In Contradiction.* Oxford: Oxford University Press.

Putnam, H. (2012). *Philosophy in an Age of Science: Physics, Mathematics, and Skepticism.* Cambridge, Massachusetts: Harvard University Press.

Putnam, H. (1975). The Meaning of "Meaning." *Minnesota Studies in the Philosophy of Science 7,* pp. 131–193.

Quine, W. V. (1948). *On what there is.* Washington, D.C.: Catholic University of America, Philosophy Education Society.

Quine, W. V. (1943). Notes on Existence and Necessity. *Journal of Philosophy 40* (5) pp. 113–127.

Rank, O. (1998). *Psychology and the Soul: a study of the origin, conceptual evolution, and nature of the soul* (G. C. Richter & E. James Lieberman, Trans.). Baltimore: Johns Hopkins University Press.

Ricketts, E. (2006). Breaking Through: Essays, Journals, and Travelogues of Edward F. Ricketts. In Rodger, K. A. (Ed.), *Essay on Non-Teleological Thinking.* Oakland: University of California Press, pp. 119–134.

Ricoeur, P. (2003). *The Rule of Metaphor: The Creation of Meaning in Language* (R. Czerny, K. McLaughlin & J. Costello Trans.). London: Routledge.

Ricoeur, P. (1990a). *Time and Narrative, Volume 1: v. 1* (K. McLaughlin & D. Pellauer Trans.). Chicago: University of Chicago Press.

Ricoeur, P. (1990b). *Time and Narrative, Volume 2: v. 2* (K. McLaughlin & D. Pellauer Trans.). Chicago: University of Chicago Press.

Rorty, R. (2002). *The Linguistic Turn: essays in philosophical method; with two retrospective essays.* Chicago: University of Chicago Press.

Roubiczek, P. (1952). *Thinking in Opposites, an Investigation of the Nature of Man as Revealed by the Nature of Thinking.* London: Routledge and Kegan Paul.

Rūmī, J. al-Dīn, (2008). *The Masnavi: book one.* Oxford: Oxford University Press.

Russell, B. (1967) 1902 Letter to Frege. In: J. V. Heijenoort (Ed.), *From Frege to Godel* (pp. 124–125). Cambridge, Massachusetts: Harvard University Press.

Sartre, J.P. (1992). *Being and Nothingness.* New York: Washington Square Press.

Sartwell, C. (1992). Why Knowledge Is Merely True Belief. *Journal of Philosophy 89* (4), pp. 167–180.

Saussure, F. de, (1964). *Course in General Linguistics* (W. Baskin, trans.). London: Owen.

Scheler, M. (2013). *Problems of a Sociology of Knowledge.* London: Routledge.

Schopenhauer, A. (2007). *The Essays of Schopenhauer: Studies in Pessimism* (T. Bailey Saunders, Trans.). Scotts Valley, California: CreateSpace Independent Publishing Platform.

Schopenhauer, A. (1969). *The World as Will and Representation* (E. F. J. Payne, Trans.). New York: Dover Publications.

Schrag, C. O. (2003). *Communicative Praxis and the Space of Subjectivity.* West Lafayette, Indiana: Purdue University Press.

Schrodinger, E. (2012). *What is Life?: With mind and matter and autobiographical sketches.* Cambridge: Cambridge University Press.

Serres, M. (2008). *The Five Senses: a philosophy of mingled bodies* (M. Sankey & P. Cowley, Trans). London: Continuum.

Sextus Empiricus. (2000). *Outlines of Pyrrhonism* (J Annas & J. Barnes, Trans.). Cambridge: Cambridge University Press.

Shklar, J. N. (2004). *Squaring the Hermeneutic Circle. Social Research* 71 (3), pp. 655–678.

Simmel, G. (2015). *The View of Life: Four Metaphysical Essays with Journal Aphorisms* (D. N. Levine & J. A. Y. Andrews, trans.). Chicago: University of Chicago Press.

Simondon, G. (2007). *L'individuation Psychique et Collective.* Paris: Edition Aubiers.

Smolin, L. (2019). *Einstein's Unfinished Revolution: The search for what lies beyond the quantum.* London: Penguin.

Spengler, O. (1980). *The Decline of the West. Vol. 1 Vol. 1* (C. F. Atkinson, Trans.). London: Allen & Unwin.

Spinoza, B. de, (1996). *Ethics* (E. Curley, Trans.). London: Penguin Classics.

Stambovsky, P. (1996). *Myth and the Limits of Reason.* Amsterdam: Rodopi.

Strawson, G. (2010). *Freedom and Belief.* Oxford: Oxford University Press.

Strawson, G. (2006). *Consciousness and its Place in Nature: does physicalism entail panpsychism.* Exeter: Imprint-Academic.

Tarski, A. (1956). The Concept of Truth in Formalized Languages (J. H. Woodger, Trans.). In Tarski, A. (Ed.), *Logic, Semantics and Meta-mathematics* (pp. 152–278). Oxford: Clarendon Press.

Thacker, E. (2011). *In the Dust of This Planet.* Alresford: Zero Books.

Timofeeva, O. (2018). *The History of Animals: A Philosophy.* London: Bloomsbury Publishing.

Tinbergen, N. (1951). *The study of instinct.* Oxford: Clarendon Press.

Tomkins, S. S. (1992). *Affect, imagery, consciousness. Vol. 1.* New York: Springer.

Venn, J. (2014). *On the Diagrammatic and Mechanical Representation of Propositions and Reasonings.* London: Taylor & Francis.

Von Uexkull, J. (2009). The Theory of Meaning. *Semiotica 42* (1) pp. 25–79. [https://doi.org/10.1515/semi.1982.42.1.25]

Weber, M. (1997). Science as a Vocation (H. H. Gerth & C. W. Mills, Trans.). In Tauber, A. I. (Ed.), *Science and the Quest for Reality, Main Trends of the Modern World* (pp. 382–394) London: Palgrave Macmillan. [https://doi.org/10.1007/978-1-349-25249-7_17]

Weber, M. (1949). The "Objectivity" of Sociological and Socio-political Knowledge (E. A. Shils & H. A. Finch, Trans.). In Shills, E. A. & Finch H. A. (Eds.), *Max Weber on the Methodology of the Social Sciences* (pp. 49–112). Glencoe Illinois: The Free Press of Glencoe.

Whitehead, A. N. (2015). *The Concept of Nature: Tarner Lectures.* Cambridge: Cambridge University Press.

Wolfendale, P. (2019). *Object-Oriented Philosophy: The Noumenon's New Clothes.* Falmouth: Urbanomic.

Yerkes, R. M. & Dodson, J. D. (1908). The Relation of Strength of Stimulus to Rapidity of Habit-Formation. *Journal of Comparative Neurology and Psychology* 19 (5) pp. 459–482. [https://doi.org/10.1002/cne.920180503]

Zamora, D. & Behrent, M. C. (Eds.). (2015). *Foucault and Neoliberalism.* Cambridge: Polity Press.

Zantvoort, B. (2015). Speculating on the Absolute: on Hegel and Meillassoux. In Gironi, F., Austin, M., Jackson, R. (Eds.), *Speculations VI* (pp. 79–120). Goleta, North Charleston: Punctum Books.

Žižek, S. (2012). *Less Than Nothing: Hegel and the Shadow of Dialectical Materialism.* London: Verso.

# Index

## A

Absurdity, 24, 33, 50, 59
Actor Network Theory, 50, 96, 97
Affect, 17
Alien intelligence, 82
Analis School, 55
Analytic philosophy, xi, 16, 32, 46, 64
Antonym, v, viii, ix, xi, xii, xiii
Aristotle, vi, vii, 7, 8, 17, 35, 46, 50, 53, 64, 84, 98, 100, 107, 113
Artificial intelligence, 82
Autopoiesis, 72
Axiology, 40

## B

Binary, vi, vii, xii, xiii, 5, 11
Boolean, vi, 5

## C

Capitalism, 83
Circumplex, 19, 20
Collective unconscious, 2, 52, 69
Colour, 9, 11, 14, 19, 20, 39, 65, 68, 102, 112
Communicology, 71
Consciousness, 2, 18, 19, 22, 33, 46, 65, 68, 69, 72, 73, 74, 75, 111
  Subconscious, 43
  The hard problem of, 2, 68
  The unconscious, 69
Continental philosophy, xi, 32, 42, 47, 71, 78, 80, 104
Contingency, 43, 46, 59, 70, 71, 84

Contradiction, vii, viii, ix, x, 3, 18, 26, 27, 28, 32, 35, 36, 37, 38, 39, 42, 43, 44, 48, 50, 51, 56, 59, 72, 76, 78, 81, 82, 83, 85, 86, 88, 89, 91, 96, 97, 100, 104, 107, 108, 109, 110, 113
Copenhagen interpretation, 101
Copernican revolution, 88
Correlationalism, 43, 45, 81
Cosmism, 80
Cynicism, 50, 113

## D

Darwin, 18, 22, 89, 92
Deconstruction, vi, 72
Descartes, 19, 60, 72, 77, 80, 82, 86
Determinism, 61, 71, 77, 91
Dialectic, v, vi, vii, viii, x, xv, 3, 4, 5, 16, 17, 30, 40, 46, 47, 52, 56, 73, 77, 78, 82, 83, 89, 93, 98, 99, 104, 107, 113, 114
Dialetheism, vii, 27
Disenchantment, 52, 75, 115
Dogmatism, 113
Dualism, vi, vii, xi, 4, 13, 22, 32, 42, 48, 61, 65, 74, 76, 78, 80, 83, 89, 107, 108

## E

Electromagnetic, 2, 9, 14, 17, 68
Empiricism, xi, xiv, 18, 23, 26, 32, 33, 42, 44, 60, 83, 90, 111
Energy, 64
Enlightenment, 18, 23, 32, 52, 73, 103, 113
Environmentalism, 88, 114

Epistemology, xi, 32, 104, 112
Euler diagram, 1
Evolution, 89, 90, 91, 92, 93, 104,
    114
Excluded middle, vii, 109
Existentialism, 45, 86, 90

**F**

Falsification, 37, 46, 100
Fibonacci sequence, 77
Fideism, xii, 37, 113
First principle, 77, 78, 80, 86
Fractals, 5, 9, 10, 11, 12, 110
Free will, 61

**G**

Gadamer, 8, 52
God, 84
God eye view, 56, 71
Golden ratio, 77, 109
Golden rule, 101
Gothicism, 88

**H**

Hegel, v, x, xvi, 16, 23, 26, 27, 31,
    32, 44, 46, 51, 62, 71, 82, 83, 89,
    93, 104, 110, 114
Heidegger, xi, 8, 18, 61, 62, 72, 78,
    104
Heisenberg's uncertainty
    principle, 60, 65, 113
Hermeneutics, xi, 8, 15
    Hermeneutic loop, xvi, 8
Humanism, 80, 81, 82, 86, 89, 103
    Post humanism, 82, 86
Hume, 18, 37, 38, 40, 59

**I**

Idealism, viii, x, xiii, xiv, 17, 26, 33,
    43, 44, 45, 46, 61, 73, 82, 83, 85,
    89, 93, 97, 114
Ideology, 54, 56, 82, 93, 96, 114
Incompleteness theorem, viii, 3
Infinity, ix, xiv, 28, 39, 43, 47, 60,
    66, 69, 70, 81, 102, 109, 110
    Infinite, ix, 3, 11, 13, 15, 16, 19,
    20, 26, 28, 29, 32, 39, 43, 44,
    51, 52, 56, 59, 60, 61, 65, 66,
    69, 70, 71, 74, 77, 84, 91, 96,
    100, 102, 103, 109, 111, 115,
    116

**J**

Jung, 2, 69, 80, 95

**K**

Kant, viii, xiii, 26, 27, 37, 51, 59, 71,
    72, 100, 101, 110, 113

**L**

Liar's paradox, viii
Linguistic turn, 48
Locke, ix, 42, 60

**M**

Mathematics, vi, viii, 2, 50, 58, 59,
    72, 110, 111
Meaninglessness, xiv, 49, 50, 66,
    97, 102, 115
Metaphysics, v, xi, xii, xv, 31, 72,
    73, 83, 107, 109, 111
*Mis en abyme*, 39
modal logic, viii, 28
Monism, xv, xvi, 65, 74, 76, 108
Music, 9, 16, 20, 65, 70, 102, 112

# N

Negative existential, vii, 29, 76
Neuroscience, 2, 18, 68
Newton, 1, 100
Nihilism, 51, 54, 77, 89, 102
Nothingness, vii, x, 3, 44, 50, 51,
    62, 75, 76, 77, 103

# O

Object oriented ontology, 42, 44,
    71, 72
Objectivity, 41, 42, 60, 93
Occam's razor, 100

# P

Panpsychism, 74
Paradox of the basins, ix
Pauli Exclusion Principle, 65
Perspectivism, vii, 34, 50, 72
Philosophy of communication, vii,
    48
Pi, 39, 50, 59, 109
Plato, v, xii, 2, 17, 19, 47, 55, 65, 95,
    98, 108, 110
Positivism, 23, 96
Post modernism, 50, 52, 111
Post-structuralism, vi, 34, 43, 64,
    80, 82, 96
Pragmatism, 37, 42, 48, 55, 61, 84,
    104
Principle of the identity of
    indiscernibles, 28
Process philosophy, 34, 55, 71, 90,
    97
Ptolemy, 88, 100

# R

Ramsey's theorem, 58
Randomness, 39, 58, 59, 71

# Realism

Realism, xi, xiv, 17, 43, 45, 53, 54,
    55, 71, 72, 81, 96
  Speculative realism, 33, 42, 54,
    64, 81, 90
Recursion, v, xv, 3, 5, 16, 27, 38, 48,
    51, 52, 60, 111, 114
Rhetoric, v, vi, vii, viii, x, xv, 5, 17,
    30, 40, 47, 56, 73, 77, 78, 93, 98,
    99, 107, 113
Rhizome, vi
Romanticism, 88
Russell's paradox, 63

# S

Scepticism, x, 38, 46, 50, 113
Scholastics, 47
Science wars, 32
Semantics, xi, xvi, 15, 47
Semiotics, 3, 15, 47, 71
Sociological imagination, 97
Socratic paradox, 110
Speculative materialism, 97, 105
Spirit, 52, 73, 79, 82, 83, 86, 103
Structuralism, 2, 47, 95
Subjectivity, 38, 41, 42, 60, 61, 82,
    83, 84, 85, 93, 100, 103
Sufficient reason, 38

# T

Teleology, 80, 82, 83, 85, 90, 113
Teleonomy, 90
Things in themselves, viii, ix, 33,
    42, 43
Trivialism, 113
Twelve (significance of), v, 5, 7, 14,
    16, 26, 39

# U

Umwelt, 89

Uncanny, 69
Universal grammar, 2, 34, 51, 71

## V

Venn diagram, 1

## W

Weak Pinsker conjecture, 58
Will, 61, 73, 90, 91, 93

www.ingramcontent.com/pod-product-compliance
Lightning Source LLC
Chambersburg PA
CBHW071132280326
41935CB00010B/1195